Shifting Sand

Journal of a cub archaeologist
Palestine 1964

Julian Berry

ARCHAEOPRESS PUBLISHING LTD
Gordon House
276 Banbury Road
Oxford OX2 7ED
www.archaeopress.com

Archaeological Lives

ISBN 978 1 78491 659 6
ISBN 978 1 78491 660 2 (e-Pdf)

© Archaeopress and J Berry 2017

Cover: A montage of photographs taken by the author during his time in Palestine in 1964
Back Cover: A photograph of the author taken a few years after he returned from Palestine

All opinions expressed in this book are the author's own and
do not necessarily reflect those of the publisher.

All rights reserved. No part of this book may be reproduced, in any form or
by any means, electronic, mechanical, photocopying or otherwise,
without the prior written permission of the copyright owners.

Printed in England by Holywell Press, Oxford
This book is available direct from Archaeopress or from our website www.archaeopress.com

Contents

Foreword 1

Introduction 3

Diary Entries, 1964 7

Scrapbook Letters 77

The Frankens and the Purpose of the Dig at Deir Alla 79

The Deir Alla Tablets and Plaster Inscription 83

Postscript 89

Foreword

It is fifty years since the call of Palestinian archaeology summoned me, and by some quirk of conditioning I kept a diary of my time on an archaeological expedition in the Jordan valley, and of my travels in Jordan, Lebanon, and Syria.

It is hard to believe that a youth of seventeen could in those days travel, often alone and sometimes with friends, around an area much of which is now a battlefield, and other parts considered too risky for foreign visitors.

The reason for unearthing the diary is simple; Palestine has changed so radically in those fifty years from an area largely at peace with itself, with a benign climate for much of the year, and a deep and enduring civilisation, to one of political turmoil, bloodshed, and iconoclasm.

The obstacles to Palestine returning to its happier condition are entirely human; tribalism, religious bigotry, and global agoraphobia.

I hope that this diary will serve to remind readers, to some degree, of the prize that the end of the present conflicts could deliver.

It may also help enthuse other tentative young archaeologists with a desire to take up the trowel.

My thanks are due particularly to Dr Henk Franken, the dig Director, and his wife Anne for all their support and patience whilst on the dig, and to my fellow archaeologists, mainly Dutch, who provided such enjoyable company. I would also like to thank my wife Susan for her encouragement during my many hours of writing in the garden studio, Dr David Davison for suggesting many areas where the journal could be better explained, Stephen Ashley for encouragement to produce the book, my daughter Georgia for helping editorially, and my son Albert for assisting with the photography.

Introduction

As in much of the rest of my life, no decision was required.

I was walking with my father on the downs between Compton Chamberlayne and Broad Chalke in Wiltshire, when we came across a round barrow undergoing excavation. At our moment of arrival, on a warm sunny afternoon, the archaeologists had found what they were looking for, an Early Bronze Age Beaker drinking vessel next to the remains of someone interred 4000 or more years ago. At that moment I had no idea about Beaker people, only the faintest glimmer of an understanding about the Bronze Age, but no question in my mind that I wanted to be an archaeologist.

I cannot remember when or where my interest in archaeology started; there was no specific encouragement at school,[1] and the fascination seems

An example drinking vessel from the Beaker period similar to the one found on the Wiltshire downs

---

[1] This was strange as in fact Winchester College had in previous generations educated some formidable archaeologists including Francis Cranmer Penrose, David George Hogarth, Sir John Linton Myres, and John Devitt Stringfellow Pendlebury. However they were classicists and my studies were mostly of physics and maths.

to have mainly come from within. It was encouraged by my father who liked walking on the downs and finding iron age forts.

Opportunities for getting 'entrenched' were not great for a public-school boy, incarcerated for much of the year, but I did manage to secure a spell excavating a Roman villa site near Wylye and immersed myself in such irresistible tomes as 'Crusader Castles' by T.E. Lawrence.

We also lived near the Pitt Rivers Collection before it was moved to the University of Oxford, and that was one of my favourite places to visit, avoiding if possible the collection of shrunken heads.

Before school ended in December 1963, (I had nine months until I was due to go up to Oxford), I decided to be bold and write a letter to Sir Mortimer Wheeler, then Director of the British Institute of Archaeology in London with its headquarters in the buildings of the Royal Academy. I explained that I had a deep love of archaeology, wanted to work in the Middle East, and could live off locusts and honey. To my astonishment a reply came back by return inviting me to come to his office.

I was met by a lion of a man sitting behind a vast and ornate desk. Sir Mortimer was in his day the human embodiment of archaeology, famous for his digs in Verulamium and Maiden Castle, renowned as broadcaster, and, as I later found out, a committed Casanova.

He had decided to come to my rescue: 'Well Berry, there are two decent digs going on at the moment in Palestine and I will send them both a telegram and let you know if I get a response'. Interview over in a few minutes, a very pretty secretary ushered me out, and I had time to wonder why he had given me such a break. Perhaps, unlike Winston Churchill, he liked Wykehamists.

SIR MORTIMER WHEELER

Two days later the phone went and I was summoned back. 'One dig has offered you a place. It's run by a clever Dutchman Dr Henk Franken, it's looking to develop a dating system for the Bronze and Iron ages based on the very detailed analysis of the stratigraphy of pottery remains, and it's in the Jordan valley quite near the river. There's very little pay and you will have to fund your own air flights. Do you want to take it?'

'Of course' I replied with no idea how I was going to fund the flights but with a soaring sense of excitement. Fortunately, my father was in a good mood when he came home from work that night, the flights were booked, and I could immerse myself in 'Seven Pillars of Wisdom' and other essential reading for would be Bedouins.

Diary Entries, 1964

Dutch Excavation Camp, Deir Alla – 2 Feb

Starting at Salisbury Station was strangely and sadly unromantic; only memories of waking and a premonition of a day's bustle to come. I was not feeling sad about deserting England for four months and not even slightly alarmed about my desire to escape it. Jordan was still an ideal, not a place. My parents seemed more stirred at what was taking place than I did. Perhaps the continual trivia of slight disagreements had made me insensitive to them.

The train journey lost itself quickly in magazines and the amusement of looking at new faces. I prefer the unattractive ones; they have more depth and one can afford to look at them more closely.

In 1963 a BOAC flight from London to Amman stopped at Rome and Brindisi on the way, and took seven hours. In this case, we had to make an additional stop at Damascus to let off a group of expert oil well firefighters.

Sunset arriving over Rome was beautiful; a stratified colour chart of pinky red and a peculiar green which I hear is common from an aeroplane. I was in half a mind to try to contact Gianni Pappa or Nicoletta[2] during the 50 minutes I was there, but let myself bask in its almost choking memories instead.

Two Italian film stars got off our plane which added, with their entourage of photographers, a touch of pleasant, unreal glamour.

A slightly delayed take off, and a long but rather exhilarating wait in Damascus. It was an unplanned landing, but it gave me a taste of the Arabs and I loved it. They are so strikingly elegant; a race of kings dressed up as peasants.

Arrived at Amman feeling exhausted but content at 3.00am local time, 1.00am in the morning our time. Franken and his wife were waiting happily! A sure sign that England was far behind. He has a thin aesthetic face and the straight brushed back hair of an English butler. His clothes were utterly casual and used looking, but he had a glorious decorated sheepskin waistcoat. His wife was waiting in the car; jolly and English, and dressed in rather dumpy Marks and Sparks. We set off at once through Amman which is big and similar to modern Athens; perhaps a touch scruffier but it looked

---

[2] Two Italian friends whom I had met the previous summer and who lived in Rome

sinister and exciting at night. Franken drove us in his well-worn Mercedes and the countryside appeared rather Greek. The temperature was 45° F.

We were heading to a small village in the Jordan valley called Deir Alla. It's 30 miles North West of Amman, and on the East side of the Jordan River. The site being excavated was a large tell or hill, entirely man made from the successive collapse of mud brick buildings.

Arrived at the camp at 4.30am and were met by a huge gleaming Negro with a kerosene lamp. It borders on a mud brick village. (I will describe it and my impressions another day).

Slept until 10.00am and woke feeling fresh and extremely inquisitive. Total excitement and anticipation gripped me, as perhaps they did when I was drinking tea in the Frankens' tent late the night before. I had crawled into bed with two slumbering bodies in the other part of the tent, which were gone by this time.

Breakfasted in the factory tent (sorting and sticking together of sherds and recording of information goes on there) off Nescafe and Arab bread and butter which is wholesome but tough.

Mrs Franken, who incredibly for her vitality, is disabled and lives in a wheel chair. She introduced me thoroughly to the various Dutch members of the dig team, who all thank God spoke English. More of them later. The morning until lunch at 1200 was spent wandering slightly forlornly over the tell. Everybody seemed a little too busy or shy at first to show me much, but soon the Arab sun thawed things out.

Lunch of curry, eggs, and oranges and back to the tell for the afternoon. Tea at 4.00pm and now to writing my diary. An Arab boy came up to sell me a heavenly bunch of daffodils, and the Arabs in the next door tent have a blazing transistor radio. Jordan seems all contrasts; I must stop writing as it is dark already; only 5.30.

Dutch Excavation Camp, Deir Alla – 3 Feb Monday

The first inklings of the next two months' routine are starting to arrive; strangely they are pleasant, although fixed. The camp is on the edge of a little mud-hut village, called Deir 'Alla. The construction of a house is simple; rectangular blocks of mud and straw baked into clay bricks, built up into a single room of about eight foot high. The windows are small, high up, and usually filled in with the remains of wooden tomato boxes (this fruit is the main local industry at this time of year). There is often a courtyard in front made of a waist high wall in which a few mangy chickens or goats live.

Position of Deir Alla in relation to Amman and the Jordan Valley

THE MAIN STREET IN DEIR ALLA

In all I imagine there are about thirty buildings of various shapes and sizes, and the whole has a rather brown appearance and scruffy smell. The camp is at the North end of the village, nearest to the tell, which starts forty yards away, and rises to about 100ft. It is about 200 yards from one side to the other and the excavation is again on the North side of the Tell. From the camp nothing can be seen of it, which allows one pleasantly to escape in the evenings from the feeling of work.

On the West side of the camp there is an agricultural institute which is better planned with beautiful cypresses and eucalyptus trees; they are the first thing one sees, above our permanent kitchen/canteen block, on waking in the morning.

At the moment, the Moslems are celebrating 'Ramadan' which involves fasting for a month from sunrise to sunset and drinking no water in the day. They take this as the course of nature, and make no effort to flinch from it. To fit in with their way of living we are called at 7.00am, have breakfast at 7.30am and start work at 8.00am. The Arabs work steadily until 2.00pm while we have lunch from 12.00-12.30pm. All work stops at 2.00pm, and after about an hour of sorting finds and writing notes we are free. Washing is from buckets of hot-water, looking murky-brown before we start, that is carried in to us before breakfast, and after tea.

THE POT WASHER IN HIS TENT

We seem to have a large number of waiters/cooks/hangers on in the camp; perhaps as many as six but it is difficult to tell. I am in a tent with a charming, friendly-bear-looking art student[3] who is the camp's draughtsman, and a tall rather serious archaeological graduate[4] who is Dutch. The tent is white, dirty, and large. There is ample headroom at the centre and room for three beds, as well as our shelves for storing possessions made of the usual tomato boxes. The beds are iron and feel like it, but we have lots of grey blankets to cope with the rather windy weather. On our left is an identical tent full of Arabs with loud radios during the day, and even worse snores at night. On our right (this as things are, lying in bed and looking West) is the girls' tent. Two are archaeological students and jolly, one is the housekeeper and rather awkward, all are plain.

There are four or five single man tents occupied by a pot-washer, a Department of Archaeology official who watches over us on our dig, and a middle-aged archaeologist.[5] The Frankens have a rather newer tent the same size as ours, which they succeed in making appear comfortable.

[3] Terry Ball
[4] J.A.Bakker
[5] J.Kalsbeek, our expert in ceramics

On Sunday evening the Frankens gave me a section[6] to look after; it is slightly away from the main excavation, and we hope free from anything beyond tumble-down masonry mud-bricks. I have about eight Arabs digging and the object is to reach right down to the natural hill underneath; understanding as we go the stratigraphy which is more complicated in the rest of the excavation. It is a simple relaxing job which today I have enjoyed enormously. When the digging stopped, I tried to walk to a nearby tell, but after fifty minutes I had to return. Distances in the valley, which is as flat as Holland, are hard to judge. Tea is at 4.00pm and we eat it, like all the meals, around a big table in a separate tent. Supper is at 7.00pm and lit by Tilley lamps which I enjoy.

Dutch Excavation Camp, Deir Alla – 4 Feb Tuesday

Waking was hard this morning after another night of rain, and the first inklings of rebellion stirred inside me; fortunately, this time it is nothing deeper than laziness, and soon cured by a porridge and scrambled egg breakfast.

The Arabs on the tell began to accept me more and stared less; a sure sign of familiarity. A moment of sharing some shelter in a hailstorm under a huge army greatcoat was human, and made us all feel more sympathetic to each other; still I find it difficult to feel quite relaxed.

The night's rain had washed lime down the hill, and the sections were completely obscured; very trying as by the time I had cleaned them it started again, and Franken stopped work on the tell for the day.

Wrote slightly dragging letters to Ed[7] and Jane[8] in the first part of the day, and disappointingly no satisfaction from duty done; perhaps they were not good enough.

Afterwards I took a series of pictures with the Leica, in gloomy light, of the tell and the camp; I would like to catch them in all moods. It is forbidden to photograph Arabs or 'places of dirt', as our village is officially called, in Jordan.

A glorious walk starting at around 4.30. We went in the opposite direction to the tell, after passing through a village similar to Deir Alla, found ourselves in a large wonderful valley with green fields so intense that they were hardly real, with a rugged blood-red river and the huge almost Indian mountains all around. The sun was setting and angry storm clouds

---

[6] A defined area of the excavation which was dug with straight sided walls
[7] Ed Marsden was a very close school friend with whom I subsequently started a letterpress book printing company.
[8] Jane Bristowe was an older friend from London

filled the sky; looking back to the village we had passed we found it black and silhouetted brilliantly on its little rise. A farmer was driving his herd of bullocks home on the horizon and the whole scene cried desperately for a camera; I cried too.

This afternoon I heard that at the end of Ramadan, in about two weeks' time, we have a week's holiday. I am planning to spend it in Jerusalem with Onno[9] an art student; the others know it too well and are going to Aqaba, but beaches don't interest me at the moment; life is too intense and anyway I can wait until Corfu.[10]

The cook has left after a wonderful telegram from his master calling him Saint Mohammed, but the food shows no sign of deteriorating. The evenings are too full of chatter to write any more.

A word about the team; there were fourteen Dutch members including myself and up to seventy Arabs helping on the site. The Arab excavators were divided into the six pick-men, who were the most skilled, and many of whom had previously excavated at Jericho; the hoe-men who did most of the heavy work, and eight or so basket boys who removed rubbish. All their wages were set by the Jordanian Department of Antiquities so there were no arguments about pay.

In the camp we had six members of staff; two cooks, a house boy, a washerwoman, a boy with donkey to collect water, and a night watchman.

Generally, we stuck to a fixed daily routine:
- Tea and sandwiches at 6.45
- Work 7.30 to 9.30
- Breakfast 9.30 to 10.00
- Work 10.00 to 12.30
- Lunch 12.30 to 1.30
- Work 1.30 to 4.30
- Tea 4.30
- Supper 7.00
- After supper voluntary tent work like sticking pots
- Lights out and silence 9.30

Each week we had Friday off.

Dutch Excavation Camp, Deir Alla – 5 Feb Wednesday

Strong sounds of Dutch and Arabic from the other tents, but I am very happy to sink into bed early tonight. Despite rumours of Anne's snappiness,

---
[9] Onno Cosijn, the second camp draughtsman
[10] I had arranged to meet my parents the at the end of the dig

I have found her quite charming; apparently, she has gone blind in one eye during this season's digging, but from her cheerfulness you can hardly notice it. Henk was kind this morning, and after calling off work because of the rain, he took us on a visit to the local potter. We passed about five Bedouin camps in the foothills on the way; returning when the rain had stopped, a lot were out shepherding flocks of mixed black and white sheep that look more like boulders in the rocky country. Half a mile from the town we met a river flowing across the road with bare legged Arab road menders paddling around in it. The local bus went through it but Henk left the car on the near side and we waded across. The erosion in the country is ghastly when it rains hard, and a substantial river can cut its way through the soil in a few hours.

The town was large, and mainly composed of penniless refugees. There seemed to be no big buildings except a mosque that was left half-finished to avoid taxes, and they were all of the mud-brick type.

The pottery was rambling and very muddy, but we visited a few rooms of drying pots (mainly for water and between 18" and 3'6"); and saw the ovens (kilns) that are sunk into the ground for insulation, and burn the offcuts they source from a factory making rubber sandals. Finally, we were given a demonstration by a Turk, who produced 20 pots in half an hour. They were all small and came successively from the same large piece of clay that is shaped like a sugar loaf; he worked fast, but gave the impression that a little less speed would eliminate a lot of crudity. We returned home late for lunch after waiting while Henk, Jan Kalsbeek, and Onno had their hair cut. The local barber is full of most un-Mohammedan looking pin ups. There were lots of children walking back from school carrying satchels; but the story we heard that the native Arabs had stoned a refugee, who showed he was planning to stay by planting a tree, revealed how tense the situation was here ten years ago.

In the evening I repeated yesterday's walk and took I hope 15ft. of good cine film; mainly blood red tossing water and houses silhouetted black against the stormy sunset. On the way back I was invited into the local shanty café by one of the workmen on the tell; a 'beatnik' atmosphere with mud floors, no tables, only three legged stools, and coffee brewed on a primus. The glasses were washed in front of us, literally by hand, but the result was excellent. Curious symbolic painting in

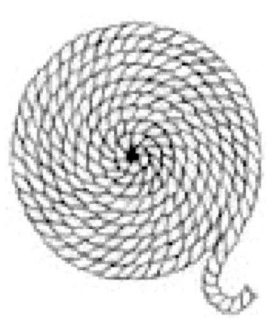

blue on the shabbily whitewashed walls, with mainly the hand symbol, and a large coil.

Conversation fell mainly to how much they all liked their wives, but they were most hospitable, and the tell workman paid the 2d for my drink which rather embarrassed me.

Onno and I were asked into the sherd washers' tent next to ours before dinner; six people sleep there but they manage to have more room and more atmosphere than ours with three; we drank their mint tea which was delicious. If there is no work tomorrow, we are going to Jerusalem for two days which will be interesting. I am anxious to buy a local sheepskin coat.

Have an idea for a cine film of a queue of people walking slowly past railings, the contrast between the camera panning with them, and against them. It is impossible to start on making a film in the Middle East as custom forbids photographing people unless you know them very well; certainly not the strangers I am looking for.

At the time, I was planning either to become an archaeologist, or a film maker, or a book printer. The film making was the most short-lived of the three options, and petered out soon after this period.

Anne asked me today to work on drawing a section (a vertically cut sand wall made as part of the excavation process that runs through different historic periods) during the Ramadan holiday and I agreed; reasons being mainly that it is simpler than saying no, I have come out here to do archaeology (not to sit in the sun in Aqaba), and this provides a good chance to learn more about the tell.

Cairo Hotel, Jerusalem – Thursday 6 Feb

At last in bed and comfortable after a rather lonely and apprehensive evening; I travelled to Jerusalem immediately after work, going to Nablus by bus with two of the girls and then on by service taxi. Arriving at Jerusalem was a bit like climbing down into a rabbit warren but already I find myself growing used to it. The city is partly subterranean and I have feeling that it becomes fascinating when one is no longer frightened of it.

A charming but over-sincere, and therefore difficult to speak to, Christian boy helped me to get to one or two shops and then insisted on taking me home to dinner. He lives in a pocket-sized house in the ancient part of Jerusalem (unconnected houses don't seem to exist in the old part of the city), and goes to school there as well. His brother is at University in Italy and his father is a teacher. He was the only member of his family (his father being out) to speak English, and so conversation and the whole proceedings were rather embarrassing.

Food was mint tea, home-made grey bread, olives, meat balls, tomatoes, sardines, and local cheese; quite safe and very good. After profound thanks, I excused myself, went to the cinema, and saw a rather gaudy but enjoyable version of Macbeth. Sadly, I was haunted by the thought of returning to the very sordid dormitory type Arab hotel where I had signed in. I met another helpful boy who was much more straightforward, and warned me that a week before a tourist staying in my hotel had been robbed of everything except the clothes he was sleeping in, and so after heavy arguments to recover the 3 shillings I had paid in advance, I came to the Cairo Hotel.

Dutch Excavation Camp – Saturday 8 Feb

The stars seem to be watching hopefully tonight from the warmth of their peaceful sky, and I have a long story to tell. Yesterday I missed writing my diary as I talked late with the Frankens, so tonight I must try to make up.

The night in the Cairo hotel was happy and damp, but I had decided to enjoy it, and this mood never really tried to leave me. In the morning there were various duties; post office, tobacconist, photographer's shop, and finally an effort to buy a nice sheepskin coat. Eventually I bought a waistcoat, and furry fashionable hat for two pounds ten shillings which seemed a fair price. The shop had some beautiful tempting Bedouin rugs which someday I would love to acquire.

Lunch in the British School of Archaeology; a very pleasant girl called Caroline there, post Oxford and 4th in history, who is attractive and I think only puts on an act of being quite mad. A rich Englishman called Malcolm Davidson rather curtailed any interesting conversation, even when it was cleverly about nothing, but the food was superb for Jordan with lots of real Camembert and the best local wine.

Afterwards a mad fight to get on the bus to Nablus or Jericho, in which I failed for not being an Arab, and had to go to Amman instead. A very uncomfortable 2½ hours, but wonderful views of the Dead Sea and the Bedouin whom I am coming to love; although their culture is quite static, what remains still makes them the most civilised, unpretending, people to look at in Jordan.

I arrived in Amman at 6.00pm, and had to hire a taxi to Deir Alla as all buses had stopped. As was expected I paid the driver half the fare in advance but after a few kilometres the taxi man stopped and used the money to buy himself a bottle of Cognac. Moslems can't hold their drink, and this made him openly homosexual and lazy; after stopping the car every few minutes in mock despair, I had to swap places to drive the taxi most of the way. He tried revoltingly to make love, and when I refused, he refused to let me go further.

After letting him drive again, he started to go fast, and purposely, in the opposite direction. I was frightened, and would have left the car if I had been sure of finding the way. Eventually when I realised where we were, I jumped out and hitched about ten miles back to camp on a tractor. The taxi man had tried to run me over but missed, and so I suppose set off back to Amman.

Arrived very shaken at the camp, and talked late. The sympathy and feeling of being 'home' was glorious.

This is an extreme example of showing the stiff upper lip in my case. Having tried to rape me the taxi man then tried to kill me by driving his Mercedes taxi straight at me after I had got out of the car. It was dark by this time and the desert on either side of the car was very flat. Every time I jumped out of the way as the car speeded towards me, the car turned slowly round again and then roared towards me. It felt as if this drama would continue until I collapsed from exhaustion, and he would have been able to run me over and destroy the evidence. Eventually the lights of a tractor appeared and I was able to flag it down and jump onto the back; the taxi disappeared into the night.

Work as usual in the morning with a warm sunny day; I must learn some more Arabic as being permanently a curiosity is wearying. We found an iron-age pit, and various interesting sections, and I enjoyed enormously the feeling of having a straightforward job to do.

After work I searched on a nearby occupied tell and on the banks of a newly dug irrigation canal for sherds or anything interesting. The local children came like a flock of sheep to help me in this mysterious game; between us we found a mass of useless fragments.

Unexpectedly at five I was asked by Franken to join a trip to Prichard's camp, which is the nearest archaeological expedition, and American. It was a little silent and awkward, but had an interesting and meaningful conversation with their draughtsman Terry; all are perturbed about how their excavation is being handled. It made me realise how much I am changing, and consolidated a lot of things which largely I forget now; love for England, fascination in people, that attitudes are a curse, that poetry is often vanity etc. Terry was full of sparks and kindness; I hear he is joining us during the holiday which will be revealing.

My consciousness about letter writing is growing, but I will let it wait until tomorrow.

Dutch Excavation camp – Sunday 9 Feb

A rather withdrawn day, and consequently unproductive; for one I missed English feelings and certainty, with the result that when Caroline, Diana Kirkbride,[11] and Ruth Black came to visit the camp I went for a long walk to avoid them; anyhow peasants never like visiting royalty!

A mood of rejection is often the most transient, and I believe the most barren; recovery is often the norm for the next day.

DIANA KIRKBRIDE

Today I suddenly felt no future in my diary, my ideas for film, for drawings, even for my friends, and I found the emptiness intolerable. A sprinkling of warm moments and the rekindling of time has lit a little fire again and I am much happier (terrible English).

I feel on the dig the whole time a pressing need to be able to speak a little Arabic and so, along with a letter home, it becomes my intention to start tomorrow. Relations with the men were casual but tiring, and the first jokes when meeting, and the sultry laughs, no longer fill the cracks.

The initiative rests with me, and the secret seems to be in appearing serious and intelligent. I hope that just recognising the problem will help; I am asked each day to the local café, and each day I have to refuse because I don't speak any Arabic which saddens me. When they stop asking it will be worse.

The pit yielded plenty of frighteningly good painted sherds, which interested everyone, and left me praying that nothing to follow would be

---

[11] Diana Kirkbride, 1915-97, worked on the excavations of Jericho from 1952 to 1955. In 1953, she began fieldwork in Jordan, including the restoration of the Jerash Theatre and excavations at Petra in 1956. During her studies of the Paleolithic and Neolithic of the area, she excavated a small rock shelter called Wadi Madamagh and made excavations at Ard Tlaili in Lebanon. She also discovered a major Neolithic site at Beidha near Petra where she led the excavations for the British School of Archaeology in Jerusalem from 1958 until 1967. Her large scale excavation of Beidha transformed our understanding of the level of sophistication of the Neolithic people in the near East.

too difficult to excavate. There were however no complete pots and hence nothing of real importance.

In my escapism, I fled for a long walk to a nearby tell after work, but was not in the mood for finding anything and was only frightened by the local camping Bedouins and their dogs. Jan Albert[12] showed me his collection of sherds picked up on odd dumps, and my appetite was whetted; perhaps to collect enough to make a mosaic with a plaster filling. Onno knows exactly how, which gives one confidence.

The usual chattering in the evening, but I spent the time reading Franken's book on Old Testament Archaeology; most reassuringly logical. In the night now, Jan and Onno are trying to sleep against the lamp, the dogs, and the snores from the Arab tent, so I must to bed.

Dutch Excavation Camp – Monday 10 Feb

A day of duties fairly averagely dealt with; a wash in the morning, and three letters to M and D, James, and David and Jill[13] in the late afternoon.

Absence has also made me hunger for sherd hunting. The morning produced some interesting painted fragments again, which Anne hopes may fit into some other pieces from the actual temple; tomorrow will tell.

One of the team, Jan Albert, is a tall, apparently rather dedicated student, who is most helpful in showing me around the tell, and explaining about the local set-up and events. He is about 26, and rather ugly with a jowl and pointed chin; inevitably he wears glasses and works carefully. I have never known him joke much, and imagine he can't be sarcastic. He studies archaeology and some branch of geology, and has no obvious peculiarities except that he is the reverse of Sipco,[14] and gets on well with him. He is gentle, and in a way paternal. He really likes antiquities, and doesn't smoke or drink much. He exudes responsibility, and evidently feels the weight of life on him; an ideal person to work with. He has just fallen for the housekeeper, an equally ugly and well balanced girl, who likes work and does it unexcitingly well. They are both Dutch. She is also tall but I imagine less intelligent if she can do a job like hers; perhaps it just has the attractive quality of something to do; would make a good nanny. They seem the type to get married, if they are not too similar, and they provide the present focus for gossip; in all ways, most pleasant, especially as one has no jealousy for either in falling in love with the other.

---
[12] Jan Albert was a Dutch member of the dig
[13] My parents are called Margaret and Derbe; David Covell is my half-brother and is married to Jill.
[14] Sipco Scholten, the dig photographer

Jan Albert

Dutch Excavation Camp – Tuesday 11 Feb

I was startled this evening to hear that Franken had been an anthropologist and missionary in Indonesia before returning to the certainty of the Near East and Europe; full of 'charming' descriptions of a man who had to guard the rotting dead bodies of a village, day and night, for three months until they were only skeletons. It seems that tigers were the worst intruders on this scene, along with vultures and body-snatchers. He also told us of his experiences spending five weeks prospecting for new archaeological sites around Jericho.

This evening five of us went to a lecture in Amman on the start of prehistoric civilisation by Diana Kirkbride, which was perhaps less technical than I had expected, but largely dispelled the traditional theory of the Fertile Crescent kindling the spark of civilisation. The photographs were good, including one of a polished skull, with an old silver and horn carved knife lying by it; perhaps a little obvious but enjoyable. There is a fascinating site in South Turkey with frescoes of vultures and dancing, on a wall, which I would like to try and visit on my way to Greece.

It now appears that the holiday starts on Thursday and that Franken does not really want me in the camp so I am planning to go to Jerusalem with the others, or at least for one or two days out of the five.

There is a lot of work on the tell with the discovery of a new Late Bronze Age pottery layer so no lack of employment, and a good excuse to avoid the slight monotony of my pit which should be finished in another four to five working days. There is still some fine painted ware coming out, but I would prefer something more structured and therefore more occupying.

A letter from my mother today which I enjoyed immensely, and so feel spurred to write more myself. Also, an attempt to learn some Arabic which went rather stickily. I hope soon to be able to write some poetry about this life as happily the old pressure builds itself again.

Dutch Excavation Camp – 12 Feb

A feeling of anticipation tonight as tomorrow we all go to Jerusalem for the Ramadan holiday – I imagine it will be rather like going to London for the coronation – but we are happy about the plan. The day's work was largely rained off, although we managed to get three hours on the tell, and I spent the morning sticking pots; an excellent cure for neurosis or frenzied thoughts, both slightly common diseases of mine.

Today Caroline from the British School came and livened things up for me by removing the warm bath of lack of social ambition and laziness. The conversation was noticeably sharper, and there was a phase of mad destruction during tea, which seemed, except for the lack of self-consciousness, rather like the Winchester days.

Prichard, the American who is excavating the nearby tell, has found some genuine museum pieces; silver plates for armour, and huge bronze bowls in a Bronze age burial site. It appears we must be excavating a very simple village.

This description could not have been less accurate as Deir Alla was in fact to turn out to be a major bronze smelting[15] centre containing finds of great sophistication! In addition, it was to provide the source of a new language on clay tablets, and had been the home of Balaam the Prophet.

I seem to write less each night but perhaps this is because camp life is becoming normal; it feels it.

Cairo Hotel, Jerusalem – 14 Feb

Two days gone before writing my diary; I can only hope that it is not a slip which evolves into a lapse, and I feel quite penitent now.

---

[15] Metal slag was found at every level, and often-rebuilt furnaces. (H.J. Franken, «The Excavations at Deir 'Allā in Jordan» *Vetus Testamentum* 10.4 [October 1960, pp. 386-393], p 389).

Feelings this evening were at the beginning quite anti-Arab, but this was probably due to my hurried leaving of the Columbia hotel. The sum effect of a smelling loo, filthy dirty public basins, even dirtier floor and room, had become too much. The Cairo is also only 8/- a night, and extremely clean and pleasant. Tomorrow morning Onno and Jan Albert move in here as well, and so there will be no loneliness.

Today I expected to be quite dull, with a bad stomach and little sleep last night; but with sufficient yoghurt, pills, boiled rice and alcohol, I feel reasonably well. In the morning Onno and I went to Bethlehem by bus, a pleasant ride and an escape from the usually rather fetid atmosphere of Jerusalem. I was feeling too ill to notice anything, but enjoyed the nativity church enormously once there. In the cellar where many suppose Jesus was born, there were pleasant carols being sung, quite snugly and safely out of tune with lots of candles and happy faces. The church was early Byzantine, basic in design without even a hint of a transept, and almost beautiful.

There was a lot of very dark mosaic restored on the walls, with vacant gaps sensibly plastered white.

Afterwards we set-out on a long walk to Herod's castle, but after a minute or two, decided to take a taxi to the foot of the mountain. We climbed up its almost too steep and because of the rain rather slippery side, in about half-an-hour; and then felt we could touch the clouds. The view of the hilly and rocky country reached for miles in every direction, with the monotony broken by scattered towns and trees.

The castle visit was a little ruined by a school tour, also arriving at the top when we did, but they kindly gave us lunch, and we managed to photograph remains, many of which may be Crusader, without too much human intrusion. An unsuccessful hitch-hike back turned into a walk, and after two and a half hours we reached Bethlehem feeling rather tired.

In the evening, after a frantic hunt around Jerusalem for everyone, we eventually landed at the British School. An excellent time spent imbibing the English atmosphere; arm chairs and very expensive glossy books littered around.

Next day was spent wandering in the sordid beauty of the Souk. We found an excellent antique shop called Baidun whose owner tries to pretend that he knows the price of everything, but charges twice as much. By much bargaining, and a backshish of Roman coins, I bought myself a B.C. Egyptian green mummy figurine which greatly took my fancy for 30/-; a fair price but a morning's work! Also I had seen some beautiful Bedouin embroidery but the price rankled and I am looking further.

The Church of the Nativity, Bethlehem; it marks the site where Jesus is supposed to have been born.

King Herod's castle and final resting place

In the afternoon, I made friends with a small Turkish jobbing printer and from this was shown around the Commercial press and the Franciscan press. Their appearance was not so chaotic as one might expect, although only the Franciscan produces good work. It is not surprising, given the wonderful rib-vaulted monastic hall they work in, and with their mountain of money. In the evening to a charming bad English film, and then apprehensively to bed.

My other love at the time, apart from archaeology, was letterpress printing. At home, I had a Dawson Payne and Elliot flat-bed press, with which with a group of friends we printed books of poems with titles like 'Green Chuckles'.

After Oxford, I went on to found with Ed Marsden the Compton Press, a printing company dedicated to using letterpress printing techniques. Over a 12-year period we printed over 500 book editions, and published over 50. What started as a small craft workshop expanded until we were employing over 20 staff, and had moved to the Old Brewery in Tisbury, Wiltshire. Our demise came with the rise of offset-litho for book production, which although much less attractive, was very much more economical as it coincided with computer aided type-setting.

Dawson Payne and Elliot flat- bed letterpress printing press

Cairo Hotel, Jerusalem – 15 Feb

An early start today, and after finding that the museum will be shut for all the time we intend to be in Jerusalem, I set off for Jericho by bus; 30 miles over very barren rocky country that passed quickly in looking.

Jericho is very much the provincial market town, but enjoyable to wander round for an hour or so. On the way in we passed a large refugee camp, and I am told that there is another one on the other side of the town. The U.N. seems to be doing excellent work, but there is absolutely no employment and the situation has been going on for far too long already; a kind of grim stalemate.

The Aquabat Jaber refugee camp was established by the UN in 1948 following the Palestine War which had created 726,000 Arab refugees (according to the United Nations Conciliation Commission published 28 December 1949). 85% of the Palestinian Arab population (of what was to become Israel) fled or were expelled from their homes.
The war started immediately after the expiry of the British Mandate on 15 May 1948, which led to a free for all between Israelis, under Ben Gurion, and the largely disorganised Arabs.
The attack on the Palestinian population had clearly been very carefully planned. The Israelis managed to clandestinely amass arms and military equipment abroad for transfer to Palestine once the British blockade was lifted.

REFUGEES FROM THE 1948 PALESTINIAN WAR

In the United States, Israeli agents purchased three B-17 bombers, one of which bombed Cairo in July 1948, some C-46 transport planes, and dozens of half-tracks which were repainted and defined as "agricultural equipment".
In Western Europe, Israeli agents amassed fifty 65mm French mountain guns, twelve 120mm mortars, ten H-35 light tanks, and a large number of half-tracks.
By approximately mid-May the Israelis had purchased 25 Avia S-199 fighters (an inferior version of the Messerschmitt ME-109), 200 heavy machine guns, 5,021 light machine guns, 24,500 rifles, and 52 million rounds of ammunition from Czechoslovakia, enough to equip all their military units although short of heavy arms.
Not surprisingly the Arabs, despite fierce resistance, were completely outgunned and had no option but to flee.

Afterwards to the Jericho tell el Sultan, that was first excavated by an American team, and then by Kathleen Kenyon. Rain had done its worst to destroy the sections and walls, but a lot remains, including twenty feet deep old city walls, and a stone tower that one can still climb inside. Perhaps the scale of the work was the most impressive, with the sections originally cut fifty feet deep, and with waste dumps the size of a coal mine's slag heap.

THE AQUABAT JABER REFUGEE CAMP OUTSIDE JERICHO

Some of the most important finds from Kathleen Kenyon's excavations of Jericho were to do with the pre and post pottery Neolithic (9500 to 6400 BC). However, it became apparent that during the Late Bronze Age, the time at which Joshua's conquest was supposed to have taken place, Jericho was not settled at all. Jericho thus joins other cities mentioned in the Biblical conquest story, like Ai and Arad west of the Jordan, and Hesbon to the east, for which no evidence of occupation or destruction has been found in this period. This is particularly interesting in the context of subsequent discoveries at Deir Alla which paint the opposite picture.

After a walk of a mile or two, to the Hisham palace.

Jericho, because of its low altitude, enjoys a very hot winter climate; about the same temperature as England in summer. Everywhere there are palm trees and orange gardens, and the place has a luxurious shield to hide the usual run down mantle of Arab towns. A Caliph in the 8th Century AD built the Hisham palace for his winter resort, in a strange Indian-Romano-Hellenistic style. It was much destroyed by an earthquake forty years after being built, and has now been largely restored. The decoration of mosaics, and intricately carved stone were quite beautiful; enough to make one long to draw them, but the structure itself, with its columns and walls was crude; the rooms are too small and the columns too massive together for their height.

Mosaic from the Hisham Palace

I had great trouble with Arab boys who insisted on following me round, asking alternately for money, or my address in England. Eventually they left, and I realised that I had not seen anything while feeling angry; I went round again, and hope that I took most of it in. Back in cold Jerusalem, I found a nice Roman pottery medicine jar for a present, and visited my printer friend Koran in St Francis St. I must remember to send him the address of Dixons, the paper makers at Albury. He asked me to his house for a drink (he is Armenian I think) after work. His house was modern, with stone and glass doors, and they were proud of an enormous radio pick-up; also of the trashy modernity of their house, and I can only hope that I appeared stunned by the whole thing.

In the evening the warmth of meeting up with everybody, and escaping to the British School after dinner. Someone helped me with places to go to in Lebanon and Syria. I have almost certainly decided not to go down to Egypt, but to head north and see Syria, Lebanon, Turkey and Greece properly, after the dig stops.

Cairo Hotel, Jerusalem – 16 Feb

We all slept late this morning, with Jan Albert not moving, and Onno and myself lazy. Usual breakfast of leban [a form of yoghurt] in the Souk for two piasters, and afterwards a huge sandwich with fried potatoes, radishes, tomato, meatballs and everything else that's bad for one's stomach in it.

I sat in the sun outside an Arab café watching more forms of people and transport busily wandering along, than are really imaginable.

Afterwards a walk around the big temple area for the first time; it is still a feast day and so entrance to the two main mosques was forbidden, and everywhere was crowded with children, beggars, holy men, soldiers, and guides but no tourists; a glorious feeling. I found it impressive for its order, its trees, and its peace, after the rest of Jerusalem, but the buildings have left no mark on my heart; anyhow they are well photographed. Afterwards to the Wailing Wall, which was solid, but lacked the wailing as the Jews no longer come here.

In the afternoon, a walk round the Armenian quarter, but the cathedral was shut; malesh. A lot to show that buildings are what one makes of them, and I am determined to visit the area with my cine camera. In the evening I saw a terrible film.

Earlier I enquired about buying a horse to ride around Jordan after the end of the dig, and am told that the Bedouins come to sell them at the Golden Gate on Fridays.

Dutch Excavation Camp – Monday 17 Feb

A day that I discovered a new oasis in fetid Jerusalem – the British Consulate reading room. It is hopelessly paradoxical to long for the East, and once one is there to long for escape, but each day I feel more normal, more peaceful in Jerusalem. For under its mad exterior of hawkers, beggars, one eyed men, pregnant Bedouin women painfully jostled, and the endless emotional procedure called bargaining, I am starting to see another side. As Ed advised in his long letter today 'a reasonable apathy towards the disagreeable elements of life'. He stoked the fading embers rather successfully, and the old agonies of trying to write or draw something well are on me again; my efforts are too spasmodic, and the results too difficult, to be able to produce anything with a peaceful heart; certainly not a portrait of Jerusalem.

Some things that made the strongest impact on me: an old poor woman sitting quite still in the crook of a wall at sunset, with her head entirely covered, and dressed all over in black; the smoke belching out of a subterranean knackers in a side street, with no light inside except the fire deep down, and a donkey baying mournfully as it was led down there to its end; a small boy dressed in tattered sacks with a wicker basket on his back, held there by a band around his forehead, collapsing with a huge load of meat into the crowd around Damascus gate, towards the end of Ramadhan; the news that in 1948 the population of Amman doubled in two weeks with the refugees from Israel; that the British community consoled itself with the idea that Arabs were childlike; the men sitting in an alcove in a Souk sewing all day, and so bow legged that they could never really walk; that one could look out of a window and see an Israeli woman feeding her child on the other side of the divide; that someone could spend an hour helping one to a hotel that wasn't queer or after getting a commission; that the next person who showed me round asked for money after five minutes.

All these impressions make the background pattern through which one wanders; I am hopelessly grasping for a true vision of real Arab life, whilst knowing that one can never understand what another man is thinking. There are moments of simple pleasure sitting in the sun, although I am the worst person for enjoying this, contrasted with the simple agony of diarrhoea in the night after eating. One's balance is upset, and it's fatalistic to try to right it in the European way.

In the morning I tried to take cine films of people walking across a square in the Armenian quarter, but ran out of film, and was not allowed onto the roof a second time; a marvellous shot missed of a basketful of bread, neatly in rows, walking from one shop to another. Goodbyes, with endless tea and coffee, to Karam the printer, and various shopkeepers. I was too frightened of Baidun to go and say goodbye to him; he is too hypnotic for a mind that likes old things.

The news is that there is no boat from Aquaba to Egypt, and so I have decided to miss it out, unless on my way back from Greece; but Alexandria, Tangier, Morocco make devastating sirens.

Reading somebody's letter from Tangier in Encounter has pricked me too; why not a letter from Jerusalem, why not a 100 poems; a thousand drawings; a golden mile of film; why not forget oneself and do all this?

The still beauty of the museum in the afternoon showed me how much I love age for its own sake. Also, perhaps it told me to love archaeology and I longed to say yes. Perhaps it is nothing more than a fine museum; it is difficult to compare what one doesn't know. Afterwards, by a multitude of discussions, to a beautiful sunset at Deir Alla, and a long letter home.

Dutch Excavation Camp – Tuesday Feb 18

Tired this evening after an early start, with a week's worth of walking and talking behind me; the sunrise was dramatically cloudy and bright, with a feeling that the sky was made of gold and cotton wool. Henk Franken decided that as it was raining all round about us, we would not work, but the weather held dry, and the camp was fraught with a feeling of waste. After a holiday, it's nice to get back to work at once.

After some writing, a long walk with Co[16] and one of the pick-men to visit a sheik's son, who had found some interesting sherd's in a field, and had brought them to the camp. He was out, but the household had a wonderfully strong Arab flavour. No women present, and we lay on a mattress without shoes, drinking endless cups of Bedouin coffee from the traditional copper pot with a long handle. We spoke through an interpreter about nothing, with the greatest seriousness, and eventually arranged to come back later.

In the afternoon, a walk by the river Zerka, with the intention of doing some drawing, but found no easy interesting subjects; I am afraid that this applies to most of the country but I must try again.

Instead I hatched a scheme for printing a book of Ed's poetry, and afterwards wrote an epistle to him. His prodding was needed and I feel much encouraged now.

---

[16] Co is Sipco, the photographer

SIPCO PHOTOGRAPHING FINDS IN THE SHADE OUTSIDE HIS HUT

The river Zerka, intersects the mountain range of Gilead, and falls into the Jordan on the east about midway between the Sea of Galilee and the Dead Sea. It was anciently called Jabbok, and formed the border of the children of Ammon. It was on the south bank of the Jabbok that the interview took place between Jacob and Esau and this river afterward became, toward its western part, the boundary between the kingdoms of Sihon and Og.

Dutch Excavation Camp – Wed 19 Feb

At last I could hold out no longer against my stomach that has been plaguing me for the last week; Jan Albert's story, that a boy who had refused to go to bed with dysentery almost died afterwards in a Jerusalem hospital, blunted my obstinacy.

The fact that my memories of the morning are so slight, that I was feeling so happy once in bed, and that I slept for hours, show that there is nothing gained in making a foolish drag out of keeping going.

My section had revealed in the morning some fascinating Chalcolithic[17] sherds, mixed up with a scattering of Late Bronze; and even though much of the work seems rather crude, their age brings glamour with it. It seems that there was a Chalcolithic deposit that was put there for a platform during

---
[17] Chalcolithic is the copper period between the Neolithic and the Bronze ages

the Late Bronze period; perhaps it was skimmed off the top of the tell to make it more flat.

The weather today has been cloudless, and many think that it is now set fair for the summer; the temperature with a slight breeze is perfect, and not yet hot enough to sap one's energy. I think that it may be almost too hot in Syria and Lebanon after the end of the dig, but I am not unduly worried by this. We have been told that the work is now certainly stopping on 20 March, and I am getting more and more thrilled at the thought of a month's nomad life after it.

I have found out an interesting amount about Rit[18] in these last few days; popular opinion holds that she is very calculating (underneath her outer layer of feminine vagueness) and takes great trouble to become a friend of everyone useful too her. She has a great failing for Roman Catholic fathers, especially Pere de Veau;[19] she appears naturally friendly although cynical about people; she writes letters with lines sloping madly in any direction, and seems to have lengthy correspondence with everyone she meets. She is the laziest archaeologist, and very clever about getting away with it; she professes not to like parties and to take detective books with her to read at them, but talks often and easily; her views seem to be intelligent but middle-of-the-way; she has a certain underlying sadness and likes the sympathy of older people, but perhaps she needs it from her own generation; she wants to get a black poodle when she gets back to Holland, but is not really suited to it; someone who is a little difficult to live with.

Dutch Excavation Camp – Thursday 20 Feb

A gentle day in bed, well drugged and feeling much more secure; midday was a little too hot, with a few too many flies; but by contrast the cool of the evening was glorious. It was superb lying with one half of the tent open, watching the colours slowly changing with the sunset, while the trees lost their green and became black against the sky. Tomorrow I hope to get up and wander gently around the camp until works starts on Saturday. I am now half way through Don Quixote and enjoying it greatly; a very rich and colourful book, and I can imagine with many interesting touches for the historian.

---

[18] I have not been able to identify Rit in the published list of team members from 1964
[19] Father Roland de Vaux OP (1903 – 1971) was a French Dominican priest who led the Catholic team that initially worked on the Dead Sea Scrolls. He was the director of the Ecole Biblique, a French Catholic Theological School in East Jerusalem, and he was charged with overseeing research on the scrolls. A leading archaeologist, who was a close friend of Kathleen Kenyon, Director of the British Institute of Archaeology in Jerusalem

FATHER ROLAND DE VAUX

Dutch Excavation Camp – Friday 21 Feb

Rice, toast, and sour tea for another day, but I was allowed up after 10 o'clock and found myself rather stronger than I expected; one's stomach feels like an empty drum, but it is preferable to a concrete mixer with rather too large lumps of gravel inside it. The morning started almost disastrously with the tent flapping everywhere, and a tiger-like wind tugging at the guys, but they all held firm. A tent never seems to be really silent, and like this, it kept any hope of sleep well away.

Everyone deserted the camp, except for myself and the Frankens, to visit Prichard's tell, and I settled comfortably down to reading Lucky Jim. It is a great relief to know that in Deir Alla one is not too remote to be reading best sellers. A pleasant book that seems like the departure of an interesting new friend when it goes. A camel spent the morning browsing peacefully over the top of Co's courtyard wall, but must have finished hungry after finding only innumerable cardboard boxes. They seem like a race that should have died out like all the other wierdities during prehistoric times, and are a little embarrassed to be still existing.

Later it broke itself loose and thundered mournfully off to the Jordan ten miles away, with a train of hysterical Arabs chasing after it. The village was very amused that anyone could be so stupid as to lose a pack camel, and its poor owner got only a very rough form of sympathy.

A thought came to me of how nice it would be to establish oneself for a few months, in a simple white washed house in Deir Alla during the winter. Co's present room is rented, including W.C. for £2 a month, and a servant can be had for 8/- a day or less. If one had something to write or paint, or escape from, it would be ideal, and even better with just one European friend. Anyway, not to daydream!

Tomorrow I start work on the tell, and will have a small pottery layer to clear, which should be fun.

Dutch Excavation Camp – Saturday Feb 22

Fascinating work with a bore in our section, a hand screw with several extension pipes; we went down eventually for five yards, and took samples all the time. Sadly, we failed to reach the clay that originally formed the base of the tell, and found only layer after layer of tipped waste.

I felt weak but better, and at last could eat normal food again. The excavation is starting to move much faster now as there is only a month left before the end of the dig, and more and more floors and pottery layers of the Late Bronze period are being found; also ovens, cerns, and bins which all help to fill in our picture of their everyday life.

The night-watchman Sucri is getting married, and for three days now there is a feast from 8 o'clock until 12; rumours of wonderful negro dancing and a blind flute player, so I must try to go. He has apparently not yet seen his wife, and only received the first stage of the dowry; no alcohol is drunk, only tea, and the women are separated from the men with the children in the middle.

A delicious fruit salad for dinner with laban;[20] something which one could easily have in England. I am reading the Huxley book Chrome Yellow which as a short novel is excellent; would appeal on all counts to M.[21]

A late evening talking mostly about people as usual, but a little on films; there seems to be quite a wave of film making among students in Holland, though their best things are documentaries of one way of life or other, and they are always hopelessly short of money. Onno seemed surprisingly up on nouvelle vogue and Dali films; it has reminded me of my old plans to hire films from the British Film Library.

---

[20] Labneh as it is often called is strained yoghurt
[21] M standing for Margaret, my mother

Dutch Excavation Camp – Feb 23

A perfect English day with pouring rain and getting demented trying to stick pots together; it seemed rather like giving someone a printing press and locking them in a room until they had printed a page of type. Certainly, not to be recommended if one has to get up at 6.30 in a prickly tent, with a hangover for it. Jan Albert was a little more boring than ever, and I suppose the stream of things I never stopped suggesting were even more insufferable; at any rate it was a change from the tell. Tonight I hope to go to the marriage feast, and so am writing early in Co's room, which always makes me jealous.

Sipco Scholten because he was the camp's photographer had been given his own mudbrick house which could double as a dark room; this became the after-hours drinking saloon for those members of the team who liked Arak and cigarettes after lights out time in the camp.

Dutch Excavation Camp – Feb 25

The wonder of living in a tent seems to be the sky, the creaks, the gales, the donkeys braying, the mud, and the feeling of cosiness that comes when the weather is bad. The mornings, and trying to wash, are the agony, and one tries to avoid both in an impossible way. Today the post came with a letter from Derbe, and one from Peter (my aunt), with an introduction to her friend in Amman, which should be useful. Dutifully I wrote home this evening, and found it an excellent medicine. I realise more and more how wonderful it is to get letters.

I am reading Kafka's book The Trial, and find it superb for provoking one's mind. It seems to be a long subtle parable that occasionally one can understand; whenever one stops reading the underlying message gleams out. Something quite over-whelming and I am longing now to read more of his work.

Yesterday it rained early, and the day was spent sticking a rather depressed pot together, and reading busily whenever the glue was drying. My section has been stopped, and so I am now helping Jan Kalsbeek on a pottery level. At times I feel it will make me a hunchback for life, but there is a definite fascination in it all. I keep hoping to find some intimate detail of L-B life, but there are only charred remains and the all too impersonal pots. Perhaps I will dream one day about it, and all will become clear.

After work, and repairing Jan Albert's bed which we dismantled last night, I filmed some of the glorious urchin village children; tattered clothes, bare feet, puddles, and no self-consciousness which together should be good for cine.

VILLAGE CHILDREN LETTING OFF STEAM

Dutch Excavation Camp – Feb 26

The contrast of a day's work in the sun, to the same when it is wet, shows me how dependant archaeology is on the weather. Today was like Europe at its best in May or June, and a little breeze kept the air from becoming sultry; the Arabs appear to be rather unconscious of any change in the weather, except as an excuse to work less, whichever way it may be.

In the morning we finished the pottery level, and were able to gloat gently at Anne and Vera[22] with forty new pots left for them to stick together. One becomes a little bored of unchanging Late Bronze age pottery, which is certainly at no time very beautiful and usually belongs to one or two basic types; still there is a great deal of satisfaction in removing a piece of ceiling that was destroyed three thousand years ago, and prying underneath.

In the afternoon drilling again, to try to discover the slope of the original tell, but every time we were stopped short by a stone. Working in a courtyard full of white rabbits and rotting vegetables, a woman came running out from one of the houses horrified at what we were doing. Half an hour's explanation hardly persuaded her that we were not undermining her house, and she stood all the time waiting for the walls to come crumbling down. All I could do was to sit innocently smiling (sympathetically, not in

---

[22] Vera Kerkhof worked with Anne Franken on repair and conservation

jest) while the two workmen explained. The difficulties arose from them not altogether knowing whether it would fall or not.

With the sunset quickly chilling the air, I finished Kafka's Trial, and went to bed early after dinner with my stomach playing up a little again.

British School of Archaeology – Feb 27

In Jerusalem for a medical check-up; perhaps dysentery? Vera came with me as she is having the same. Neither of us feel anywhere near death's door, but it seems unnecessary to have ignorance hanging over us. An uneventful day except for a charming letter from Jane;[23] staying in bed until 9.30 and working down in the camp during the morning. Am reading 'Those Barren Leaves' by Aldous Huxley. A wonderful but rather penetrating prod at literary salons.

Dutch Excavation Camp – Feb 28

No dysentery diagnosed, after a long medical session at the St George French Hospital; a terrible atmosphere and no-one seemed to mind how long one waited.

Afterwards a visit to the Archaeological museum which I found far less impressive than the last time; perhaps it was too cold, and Roman/Byzantine lacks the fascination of the Early Bronze age. Anyhow a free entry, and a guided tour round, for being a member of Franken's dig.

There seems to be a beggar who sits outside the British School every day looking as if he last shaved the week before, and rolling endless cigarettes which he is apparently well able to afford. Surely the fascination of being a beggar is that one can be a tramp or a poet? Why just a chain smoker? He camps in a pyramidical (and quite un-Arab or Bedouin) tent in the garden, and always seems absorbed by the good fortune of finding a stone to sit on. Quite unlike the women beggars who sit entirely veiled, and appear at dusk like bundles of old rags; nothing to make them human except the smell.

This evening a long talk with Anne and Henk about Durham Cathedral and casting bronze statues, which appears not to have changed much in 3000 years. I am to be put in charge of a new section next to the temple area; the aim seems to be to discover more about its ground plan, or its pottery. On the way down perhaps an iron age foundry which could be fascinating.

Tonight, the cursed South wind has come, bringing with it rain and the rather fuggy atmosphere; both are entirely understood but irritating. A splendid letter from Ed (how attractive the atmosphere of having something

---

[23] Jane Bristowe, a friend from London

to fight against can sound), and also from M, Jill (my Scottish sister in law), and the British School at Teheran.

I had been offered a semi-permanent job to join an archaeological expedition in Persia and was torn between going, and giving up or postponing my start at Oxford in the autumn. In the end Oxford won, but that decision could have changed my life.

Dutch Excavation Camp – Feb 29

A day 'borrowed from God' but a fascinating one despite the almost continuous rain. In the morning Co, Jan A and I went to Amman to try to find crates for shipping the various antiquities back to Holland. On the way an hour spent waiting for some kind of transport in the local café; impressions of three legged stools, broken down taxi drivers, crumbling white walls revealing the mudbrick behind, and the usual Primus with an enormous Victorian metal teapot on top.

Amman is a basic town, unashamedly jumbled, commercial, and unpleasant. No proper restaurants or theatres, while all the time having the impression of a huge temporary jungle.

Lunch with Aunt Peter's friend Ali Zubi who snorted frequently, spoilt us well, and ended up explaining his hatred of Jews. Anyhow a certain self-

AMMAN AS IT WAS AROUND THE PERIOD OF MY VISIT

conscious luxury that seemed glorious for one lunch. Co was there too, and avoided making my blunders about the Bedouin; Zubi has them for cousins!

Back in the afternoon through an unreal world; the sun just breaking through again onto the earth, and a view down the Jordan valley with mists and the light reflecting off the ribbon of the Zerka valley. In the evening, some Arak and a long letter to Ed.

Dutch Excavation Camp – Sunday 1 March

Letters to Peter, and Jill; great fondness for Sukri the night watchman, who gives me tea that is almost as dark as himself. A giant, who had cancer and recovered.

In the kitchen Jan Kalsbeek was sitting shaving in front of a cracked mirror imitating donkeys; in my tent Jan Albert imitates a professor.

A frantic day of finding walls, uncovering a semi-nomadic pottery level and preparing it for a photograph, finding a kaboon oven, and making drawings. Tomorrow promises the same, and time has become a comet with me floundering in its wake. In the evening some cine shots of a mule eating grass, and rubbing its neck tenderly against a donkey; tragically the donkey was not so affectionate.

A pottery jar four-foot-high costs 1/- and water jug 4p.

A brilliant moon tonight and the ground appears to be covered in snow or sand. Earlier when the moon was hidden, the stars were torches; now they are just decoration. Strong desires to spend a day or two with Ali Zubi after the end of the dig; anymore, and civilisation would pall. In Jordan it has much less appeal than mud.

Abu Simon[24] has his car back, but has to run it in again. A long chat with Anne telling me stories about Greece.

Dutch Excavation Camp – 2 March

My first plan drawing today, with all the Arab workmen breathing down my neck; I was petrified that perhaps I could not carry it off, but all went well. The semi-nomadic pottery level is regarded as important, and I try to treat the usual sherds with added respect. The fatal West wind blew strongly in the afternoon, and the distant mountains became vividly clear, but the rain held off. It is glorious to really feel the weather again. Living in the country with no real protection, it becomes something thrilling; it is also utterly variable.

---

[24] Abu Simon was an important village figurehead

Reading Snow's 'The Light and the Dark' which awakens new life in relations with people; I am still too young not to be hopelessly influenced by books, and love them as such. An evening of practical jokes, which seem rather a new game to the Dutch. Rit, with her endless writing of crooked letters, longing for someone rich and old-fashioned, is becoming to me a little pathetic; I seem to worry too much about her, and Co says it is much worse than last year. The summer's dust is starting already, and everyone is grasping at what's left of the spring, that has only another few weeks to run. It is too perfect to last.

Dutch Excavation Camp – 4 March

Early to bed for once; well washed and shaved, but with the corn-mill in my stomach still rumbling on.

At last I am really involved in my two sections, and look to them with the same reverence as going back to printing. The days, with their cold dawns and hungry sunsets, flee by; and the end of the dig seems certain to coincide with its summit.

I spent the evening wearing my white Arab kafeia, and am falling in love with this very practical head-dress. Perhaps one day I will summon the courage to wear it on the tell. I try often to spend an hour or two chatting with Anne; she seems to enjoy an English reminiscence which is much easier when Abu Simon is away. My hat has earned me the name of Abu-bis, and I find now that Co is really Sipco, and that Geetje is spelt this way.

Now that Mohamed the cook is back, we have more exotic and more deadly food; he is pleasant and I enjoy enormously my cup of tea each night in the kitchen, with the primus stove, and the Arabs sharply shadowed on the white walls. Letters to Jane, Jessie (my step-grandmother), and D&M which is a relief; strangely I enjoyed writing to Jessie the most, but perhaps one can be most honest with a mad woman. Onno stays as simple and as charming as ever, which amazes me after a month; perhaps it is due to his English being the worst.

Dutch Excavation Camp - 6 March

Arabian children seem to have three main amusements; their greatest fun is staring at foreigners with our white skin, unhealthy eyes, and too many things to do. They shout 'by-by' endlessly; they cry for backshish and point to stomachs swollen from lack of food; they stand patiently by the side of the road trying to sell old coins or Hobesi; in exasperation they throw stones and become half frightened little brigands.

The next is making hoops out of bicycle wheels with the ribs removed; they roll these down every village hill, guided patiently by a piece of strong wire with a U at the end. This becomes better fun when the street is crowded, and there are laden baskets to upset in their crazy race.

The third and most ambitious is pretending to be a taxi driver. Private cars belong only to the elite, and carry higher snob value than in Europe. The Mini-Minor could never become a favourite in Jordan; only the outdated and ship-like American cars are popular. The Dodge, Philadelphia, and Chrysler are ostentatious enough.

Service taxis flourish and heavily outnumber all other vehicles; they have green number plates, and tattered chromium insides. By paying a little more than for a bus, one has the advantage of waiting until they have seven passengers (in the Jordan valley where they have no policemen in the afternoon, this quota was often raised to eleven), of arguing endlessly how much a journey is worth, of being offered Camel cigarettes and handshakes, and of having an ardent anti-Jew sitting on one's knee questioning one about Douglas Hume's anti-Arab speech in Canada. On the whole they are the best way of travelling.

The children pretend to be steering their taxi, with a wheel made from a slice of a bicycle tyre; the quota of passengers is accumulated from those who have nothing to drive, or no hoop, or enjoy the game. The hoard moves down a road like a swarm of bees; stopping occasionally to laugh, or fight, or take turns at leadership.

Today Onno and I went first to the Amman museum, as it was a Friday and the weather uncomfortable. It's a bungalow building, outside the town, and arranged informally. A mudbrick excavated from Jericho, and some burnt Iron-age corn are neighbours to a faience jar with a cartouche seal and a crumbling bronze dagger. The room is full of no smoking notices and the inevitable stuffed camel. Nothing is really good, and most only of the 'interesting' Deir Alla standard. The Early Bronze pottery was impressive, but the place was deserted. A small provincial town museum in Jordan's biggest city.

Afterwards to Jerash, where we arrived at about half past eleven; perhaps the most beautiful place I have met yet. It was a day of contrasts; the strong sun pouring down from the grey-black sky. The monumentality of the ruin compared with its original splendour. The paint-box green eucalyptus trees growing from solemn orange walls. The modern tourist café, and the trouserless men who sprung bare-footed from behind a wall to sell us Roman coins. The long street, and the restored paving stones misplaced with the carriage ruts running haywire.

21 Jerash; the main street called Cardus Maximus which ran North South

The city of Jerash can be traced back to the Bronze Age, but was greatly enlarged and rebuilt by Alexander the Great as one of the cities of the Decapolis. It flourished under Roman rule, and was thriving until the Persian invasion of 614.

The occasional showers washed it clean of people, and half seen Romans in their sandals and white togas kept fleeting away from me around the corners. The piles of misplaced Corinthian column tops were almost as beautiful as the circular colonnaded forum. It was a day of chiaroscuro and I had a colour film! Fate walked away from me, but I photographed everything; after the thirteenth picture the sun came out.

It is senseless to repeat what is in the guide book, except to say that it is all true and more. The monumental in ruins perhaps appeals to a dangerous nature; it uplifted mine.

Dutch Excavation Camp - 7 March

First dawning of making a documentary about the excavation; a plan made during the morning's work. One is hopelessly limited with only one film and an 8mm camera, but a nice taste of things perhaps to come. The sections are almost done on the Late Bronze Age destruction level, but at the moment the work is mainly earth moving. It is better to be absorbed, but an idle day in the sun is a change; perhaps too much of a challenge to my inability to do nothing happily.

A new Danish girl arrived with Vera for the night, but she does not rank as a 'bird'. Early to bed tonight feeling rather tired.

Dutch Excavation camp – 8 March

The earth in Jordan offers us too many colours for peace; they are softened gracefully by the dust, and brought shimmering to the surface, and our notice, by the rain. Today was dry, with the sun hazily hot and the distance quivering in the heat.

It was scraping down a section for my film that really helped me see a little of this fantastic beauty; mustard yellow bricks sitting against piles of ochre and orange burnt rubble; blue grey rain deposited levels, each a subtle play against his neighbour, running up to a blue-green wall. Odd dashes of red and black lent by old fires to this strange art form. Not all of man's accidents are doomed!

On reflection, this was most probably not one of 'man's accidents' but rather the aftermath of an earthquake that had caused a fire. Our tell was sitting on a fault line and had been subject to a succession of earthquakes.

In a tell it is hard to feel any sense of tragedy. One likes a period that leaves an interpretable mess behind it, or rather beneath it. Iron-age skeletons have no awe; like their limited artefacts they are too desiccated.

As I sit a huge negro, Abu-Sakri, sings unending wordless tunes; sometimes he stops to talk or to laugh, and I start to write again. When he drinks he resembles a buffalo, but his heart is too soaked in hashish to roar. A beast of a man who drinks water sloppily by the bucketful, and is too tender to work.

The village children wander against the tell's horizon; black gawky figures gripped by the sun and sight of men digging. One or two wander down, holding hands in their effort to be nonchalant, and the rest rush after them; a bumbling avalanche of hope.

These children have already felt too much for their age; they have the eyes of a grown man before they reach ten. Life in Deir Alla is still largely a gamble, and at that age the odds are heavily against them; the fittest survive but they are universally scared. A third of the children born are dead before they grow up. The Ramadan's fasting prevents mothers from feeding their babies properly, and claims many victims. The usual course of unchecked disease does the rest.

SOME OF THE ARAB WORKMEN GETTING PREPARED IN THE MORNING

I began shooting film this morning, and have completed the sections on work on the tell. The workmen appear less frightened of cine than stills; perhaps they feel that it can only last for a moment on the screen, while a still picture takes a part of them for ever; perhaps it is just the novelty.

Dutch Excavation Camp – 9 March

A truly archaeological day, except that I succeeded in fitting in the last few chapters of Etruscan Places (D.H. Lawrence) into the gaps. I hope that we have found the fourth wall of the temple; large and burnt almost beyond recognition to a coarse red grit, that rests half seen in its surroundings of crumbled green and orange, lying amongst the debris of its upper half. Hints of significance in its new life.

Nearby an Iron Age brick lined pit was cutting decisively through another Late Bronze wall; no archaeologist in the world can know what evidence it killed and I much less. Rit has found a Middle Bronze Age pottery level deep down after feet of greenish faceless rubble; it's the first on the site and everyone is rather thrilled.

In the evening, as the sun was climbing wearily down behind the mountains, we bathed in the Zerka river; all the village decided to watch, and we had difficulty finding enough water to cover us. We walked back through the refreshing dark with the telegraph poles rearing suddenly out of the ground; the moon does not shine until nine or ten each night and there is no dusk. In the camp we had wine for dinner, in a fit of much needed extravagance; it was fizzy, local, and very nasty but at least a celebration.

Dutch Excavation Camp – 10 March

Honor Frost[25] writes to say that she is leaving for London, but Anne suggests John Carlswell to stay with in Beirut; also that we should travel from Amman to Ma'an by the local train. It takes a day to do the trip, sleeps the night at its destination, and returns the next day. To catch it further down the line one just places a car or oneself across the lines.

A long talk to Anne, hearing about their housing problems and that they would like to leave Holland, which sounds from them to be horribly conventional. Their son cannot accept the rigid C19th school teaching and is failing badly, which with academic parents must always be a problem. Henk's first wife refuses to allow him to go to an English school, and he can't bring himself to ignore her. He is 17, lives for travel, and is at the equivalent of a secondary modern.

Before dinner another swim, and we managed to avoid the hordes of children this time; just one Arab boy learning his school-work came and sat next to us, while we talked until it was dark. He was silent, and happy to be with us; perhaps he was thrilled to find some Europeans who preferred sunsets to guide books, and he didn't bother to plague us with English. The banks of the Zerka were alive with mournful sounding bull frogs, and string after string of their eggs.

Dutch Excavation Camp – 12 March

After being made senseless by sticking photographs into the Register all day, and being cheered by a letter from Peter, and a marvellous walk, and the arrival of films from Salt, I feel energetic. In a wadi nearby I found a crude possibly Iron Age pot, almost complete, in the classical squat shape with a thin neck. The water had cut clean into this little tell, and I hope tomorrow to uncover something truly exciting.

Last night there was a fierce spring storm, and we heard that thirty yards of the Amman Jerusalem road was washed away, with all the road mending equipment travelling with it. After the sun has baked the earth hard, there is

---

[25] Honor Frost (28 October 1917 – 12 September 2010) was a pioneer in the field of underwater archaeology. Professor John Carswell had been an archaeological draughtsman for Kathleen Kenyon at Jericho, and in 1956 joined the Dept. of Fine art at the American University in Beirut.

THE HIJAZ RAILWAY IN 1915; IT RAN FROM DAMASCUS TO MEDINA, AND WAS MUCH TARGETED IN THE FIRST WORLD WAR BY LAURENCE OF ARABIA.

instant flooding. A stream decided to flow under the Frankens' tent but luckily between their two beds.

We have a minute nervous servant called Abu-Abdullah who makes all the mistakes in the camp. Apparently whilst on a dig in Petra he decided to murder the Jericho pick-men with his knife; they had been teasing him and were all travelling home on a truck together. Diana Kirkbright persuaded him to say goodbye to his wife first, which he duly did. When he returned, he found that they had already set off, and for his trouble had to bus back to Amman.

On the same day Mohammed the cook heard Diana [Kirkbright] making terrible noises in her tent. He was deeply attached to her, and lay awake all night deciding how to deal with her body when she had died. He waited until it was time to bring her tea in the morning, and then walked in horrified, with three other men, expecting to carry her body out. Diana instead was quite well and had only been snoring.

The official Jordanian report on the irrigation possibilities in the country left out the area around Deir Alla because three successive parties had been murdered by Bedouin. This was in 1935.

The Jericho pick-men, when they first came here to dig, 50 kms from their homes, travelled back to the city to buy their food because this area was so foreign to them. One came to Henk and asked politely if it was alright for a Jericho man to have his washing done by a Deir Alla washerwoman.

The nails that were put in my shoes yesterday to keep the soles on are already coming out. It is the custom to make shoe bottoms from old car tyres.

THE POT

Dutch Excavation Camp – 13 March

Last night [Sip]Co and I talked until the moon had gone down behind the tell, and in an hour or two the first vague glimmerings of a new day would start. The mood of Tilley lamps and the long mournful rows of Late Bronze-age pots, produced a real traffic of ideas between us.

I put down in my diary what I recalled as the gist of the conversation. It looks as if the Arak or something stronger must have taken hold!

'We were realising how essential the deep-cut needs of men were still and how they seemed to be in vivid contrast to one's education.

Man has a deep urge to travel, after a million years spent wandering as a nomad, or in vast population migrations from one continent to another.

How the sea was always something quite special to man, and the pleasure of sailing a distillation of the old fear, and a sense of great conquest.

The crazy exhilaration from danger, something quite opposed to fear, comes from the need of man to conquer the animals in the world, and his own sub-species now extinct, to remain quite pure.

In our hearts there is something that despises difference, that shies away from eccentricity, because in our past it has spelt death; the same applies to madmen, or to sadism which has contributed so essentially to our survival. Aldous Huxley's theory of the brain filtering away the vividness of our impressions comes from the need to survive; happiness had to be momentary, rather oblique, if it did not leave us weak and careless.

The logic of a depressive fit is something which man is only just becoming able to face; the consequence is suicide and a loss in our ability to exist.

Complete catharsis is in no way confined to drama; it can come from meeting somebody for once not other, or again totally other; it can come from beauty, or music, or speed, or making love, but it is again fatal.

True religion is connected with our deepest traits; our curiosity, our need of the sun as the creator and in a human way our continual anti-position to it, our hunger, and with the spiritual catharsis it is recognising something else. Perhaps it is often a sensation of understanding how other, how distant and inconceivable our souls really are.

Education can only come in the Western sense when the real forces in life have lost their significance; it can afford us to encourage catharsis, eccentricity, vividness, peace and the new world of fatal beliefs, because even survival has become less significant. But it is the realisation of how other our basis is, of the conflict between modernistic philosophy and the real religious philosophy, and of the un-religiousness of Christianity that came from this talk. Also to realise how simply this is shown in my attempts at laziness; there is always a conflict between my intellect which says how wonderful it is to do nothing, and to forget about doing; to look at something all day in a Buddhist way, and to be entirely hedonistic.

My beliefs though are based on experience which can remember only pleasure in activity, which urges work, and planning and creation. And in myself which sensibly likes doing nothing, likes working madly when it has to, likes the warmth that comes after effort.

Also, I realised the self-consciousness that exists inside me, perhaps because of the otherness of my various selves. How I am always mentally writing what I am feeling or doing; how I sometimes think that I feel more richly if I analyse sensations to myself, and then they are of course lost;

how I can spend hours listing things, listing plans, listing footsteps in an ugly illiterate way. I can hate myself for this but it is gripping me too fast. A half consolation found in Orwell describing the same about himself; and also his loss of it like teeth, or an appendix. A little painfully, a little too unnaturally, but because he understood its uselessness.'

Today was the first Friday with a Saturday morning happiness; even the flies which regarded me sinisterly in bed, as approaching a corpse, could not eat it away.

Breakfast late, and afterwards a day spent walking to the site where King Omri[26] is supposed to have lived, where man has built his most basic temples, to an atmosphere of true religiousness.

Now there is only a hill, and the hidden paraphernalia of the past that says too much too simply. Mauve heart-shaped stones that once formed columns; poppies growing heavily round a slight depression, rims of fine old pots washed visible by the rain, and the wind that straightens one's hair. Crumbled stones with one side oddly flat. Round about the Bedouins camped, and their goats had learnt how well the grass lives on this rocky temple mound.

The walk carried us wandering through the mountains on one side of the Zerka. At first all was familiar, with the barley that in the last week had grown a beard, and the litter of our old bathing sites, and happiness. The flowers had changed a little for our coming; they were well scrubbed by the last day's storm, and the earth between them had softened to green. The river was red and angry, but one understood that it's wrath came from two nights ago, and that it still felt its need to maintain its appearances. How human to avoid a good temper when one is no longer irate, and to enjoy in the new peace one's friends' expectancy.

Once round the mountain's finger, we were into new ground. The sun had broken through the grey faceless clouds, and a beam slowly revealed the rifts on the other side. As the winds moved, one knew God's blessing was being eked into this chosen barren earth. We walked on. The path led us soon to a single red wild tulip; perhaps it always grows here and men had learnt to pass this way, or perhaps it was just the 13th of the month. It was macabre, with its pointed confident flower, and the twin rococo leaves that curled, evenly toothed, away from the earth each side.

We passed some caves that still reeked of the cattle that had spent the night in their shelter; the water poured smoothly through the roof and ran down a well-worn stalagmite to our feet. After an hour or two in the hills, we saw some tiny distant figures laden with brushwood fording the Zerka.

---

[26] King Omri was the 6th King of Israel and reigned from BC 884-873

THE ZERCA RIVER IN SPATE

With the green-black mountains behind, and the brilliant specks of their clothes, they were a human blob in a Chinese landscape painting.

Soon a mound, with an artificial cake-shaped top that is only recognisable in the distance, came near. It is almost a pyramid surrounded by the steep walls of the valley's side, and unmistakeable. We felt a sudden shudder, with the sense of Moses' tragic angel, who was rumoured to have been here, and shuffled a little more slowly towards it.

We had to leave our eyrie and cross the Zerka; some Bedouins nearby looked horrified when we took off our trousers, and half-scared and half-triumphant waded across. While holding hands, it was barely possible to touch the bottom, and we reached the other side some distance downstream. Lunch, after ceremoniously killing a scorpion that had chosen to share the only windless ledge, was delicious but meaty, and we missed a bottle of bad red wine. The remains we gave to a shepherd boy, who ate them sadly, with one hand on his dagger and the other in his mouth.

We had eaten at the foot of the mound, and I can remember little of the next hour. We wandered leaning against the wind and with the comfort of each other over this barren patch of land; we all felt its numinous awe too strongly to say much, and rather happily we started to walk back again. This time, along by the side of the river, but even the torrid water, and the sun appearing only in time to set, hardly moved us. We had had too much to be anything but limp and tired; the magic had left us quietened.

Dutch Excavation Camp – 14 March

Arabian coffee is made by boiling water once in a small conical shaped tin pan; a tablespoon of coffee and a little sugar is then added for each person. It is put back on the fire until it has boiled up, and been allowed to simmer down, three times. The tea is made in the same way, except that a few sprigs of mint are added.

It is a common belief that porcupines are dangerous animals, because they can shoot off their spikes, and when hit one will die. Similarly, if a chameleon flicks out his tongue at one. This happened to Saleb's[27] uncle, and so we are often reminded of it.

The way of keeping bees is to put the swarm in a large water pot, with a hole drilled the size of a coin through the bottom. The top is then sealed, and at the end of the year the bees are smoked out and the pot broken to take the honey.

Today Co is in bed with a high temperature and fever that brings him wonderful dreams. One was of the Pope looking like the one that Bacon painted, taking a bath on top of a skyscraper. On either side of the building were even higher skyscrapers, and along these two sides, great walls of cornflake packets were made.

He finds that when conscious he cannot really think, and is starting to worry about his condition.

A fine cheese can be made from hanging yoghurt in a muslin bag for a day or two, and it mixes well with arak. Leban, as yoghurt is called in Arabic, is very common and is often used hot as a sauce over meat and rice dishes, with special nuts on top. These are made from frying melon seeds.

Mohammed the cook had a child today, and he presented a mammoth box of chocolates to the camp; they were solid plain chocolate with nuts at the heart, and delicious.

A village tomb is made by burying the body, lying on its right shoulder and facing East, wrapped only in a sheet. A small natural stone is stuck into the ground at its head and foot. The whole graveyard looks like a green trifle with almonds stuck into the top. The hobesi grows well here, and in a practical way the goats are put out on it to graze.

Abu-Sukri has stopped wearing his blue patched Turkish trousers, and has for some reason dug much deeper into reality, and the earth of the tell. He sings less, but still cannot bring himself to do much work beyond supporting his weight and his worries. For the rest, our Arab diggers seem happy, but uncertain about the end of the dig and the loss of a steady income.

---
[27] Saleb was one of the camp staff

Dutch Excavation Camp – 15 March

At first the day drizzled, and the decision to stop work on the tell was put off until we were thoroughly drenched. Afterwards I set off with Achmed and Salib[28] to the local shoe-mender; the sky was vivid with the battle between the sun and the rain. Brilliant cornfields, which in the distance had misty pillars of a shower rising up to the sky; the usual rainbow but nearer and more tangible was reflected in the road's puddles. A few women walked past us chattering in their high-strung voices, with unnecessary water for the fields. No-one noticed the rain as the air was warm, and the sun sure to succeed in the end.

The shoemaker, a dusty man in a brown balaclava hat, which further down merged into his skin, was standing outside his shop; perhaps unconcernedly flaunting his need for customers.

The presentation of work made him more surly than he looked, and Achmed had to bargain heartily for the price of 27 piasters. The shop's inside, hardly distinguishable from the outside with the remnants of rain pouring muddily down the walls, was supposed to be white. It was one room, decorated with exhausted shoes and a huge Singer sewing machine which he had never understood how to manage. He groaned as he worked, popping bundles of tacks into his mouth and producing them singly, and facing the right way, when he needed; ripping off the old soles like bark from a tree, and sharpening a keen Turkish sword that he used for cutting the leather.

Everybody passing down the street stopped to see him with a customer for once, and I began to fear for my shoes; fortunately, a young boy soon arrived with his father's enormous Wellington boots. The shoe mender took a piece of my old heel, and sewed it carelessly over a tear.

The boy was pleased, and after handing over some tobacco for the work, stood around to watch. The cobbler had an ample supply of three legged stools for his audience, and a tomato box for himself to work from. When he sensed a little boredom in his audience, he removed a large tattered handkerchief from his finger, and showed us a scar stained red with anti-septic.

Handkerchiefs are a luxury in Deir Alla, and this impressed everyone except Achmed, more that his wound. Achmed's family run a shoe shop in Jericho, and I suppose there are certain scars that come with this trade. Our shoe-mender's wound ran all the way round the base of his thumb and was obviously festering.

After an hour or so he had finished and seemed even more angry; I gave him 30 piasters and walked the mile back to the camp most comfortably.

---

[28] Two workmen on the dig

The sun's arrival had delighted a strong white stallion which galloped carelessly past us, with a hysterical local dignitary on his back.

In the evening I finished Kenyon's fascinating book on Jericho,[29] happy to realise that descriptions of an excavation could become so readable.

The British School of Archaeology, Jerusalem – 17 March

Diana Kirkbright has decided to take me with her on a trip through the desert in April; walking and travelling by camel with some Bedu, Ali and Mohammed for company. If Laurence is right it should be a chance to see something clearly, instead of the terrible arty mauves that cut so deep into life. I will have to learn to draw, and to take archaeological photographs before then, and so imagine I will be rather confined to camp for a while.

Last night there was a party to celebrate the end of the dig; the drinks provided were as expected, but everybody felt either a little too sad, or too excited about the future, to be bothered to say anything much at the time.

Also it helps if one can go somewhere different, and with a choice of one's tent, or to mingle with Arab's drinking tea, it was hard.

A very well-known sight is of a tiny colt-like boy pushing a rusty wheelbarrow down the centre of the village; soon after avoiding one or two ruts the wheel came off, and it settled on its side like a camel. The boy sat down and cried over it, showing us a glimpse of what his toy was worth.

I wonder sometimes if it is possible for me to make any real friends among the Arabs; perhaps I am closest to Ibrahim who has not yet appeared in this diary. He is a tall half Egyptian half negro man, with curly hair and a certain knowing masterly face. He is one of the camp waiters, and lazy in the way that a lizard is; very intelligent, and can lay himself out as dead for an age in the sun. He expects no sympathy, or pretends that he does, from the camp and responds happily to any quip.

Dutch Excavation Camp – 19 March

Left Jerusalem last night with a rush of hope for the desert, and love for an C18th Persian silver embroidered cushion, and with tiredness which only ended when we reached here at 2am. Before the drive back with Anne and Henk was a filmshow of Romeo and Juliet at the British Consulate. Fun to see with the film-set versions of Padua and Mantua which were quite like the souk today, but the sound system masked any Shakespeare in it, and the suicides seemed never to end.

---

[29] *Digging Up Jericho*, London, 1957

In the day I had written a little, and wandered around Jerusalem in the rain; the same type of life as London in the sun, and I hopped from oasis to oasis to drink tea and talk a little politely. Goodbye to the funny greedy rabbit of a printer called Karam, to the pudgy Elia, and perhaps altogether to Jerusalem. It is nothing but a fairy-tale city, but a painful one, and so small that I feel conceitedly that it changes a little when I leave.

Today I fell asleep in the afternoon, and was woken only for dinner. We seem to work harder with the Deir Alla half empty, and the camp seems perfect; Co, Terry, Dominique,[30] Anne, Henk and Mohammed Juhra[31] are all that is left.

Dutch Excavation camp – 21 March

Two days of learning a little to prepare for Diana's expedition; drawing stones and flints yesterday with the wind beating the rain into the working tent, and in between the vivid sun and the rapid action of dragging everything under cover. The tents obstinately refused to leak, but the usual rivers formed themselves through the camp-site. This time avoiding the tents, but cutting their way so deeply that the ground is scarred with ditches. The dry dusty earth has none of the European resistance to water, and a wadi with high toppling banks can form after half an hour's rain shower. The farmers are frightened now of having their lush bristling crops washed out of the ground.

Two missionaries from Bali arrived, full of God but empty of any charm or apparently understanding; the man with his grey and pink face looked perfectly suited for a Bacon portrait, and his wife had legs like gun barrels. They were associates of Henk when he was still preaching in Indonesia, but kept their jobs whilst Henk lost his for being too liberal.

Climbing into bed late as usual I had some ghastly pain in my stomach that convinced me that I was about to die; looking back I am only horrified that I worked out everything so calmly despite the pain. It passed slowly after an hour and I slept fitfully in a dreamy awkward way.

Today I have been helping with the accurate surveying of the site with Terry; using a theodolite it is amazing how accurate one can be, and also a little perturbing when mud bricks are nice and haphazard. Now that Gertje has gone, the management of the camp is left for anyone who has time or is interested; an excellent system but soon we will have finished all the exotic looking cans left in the canteen and be left with rice and water, and bony village chickens.

---

[30] Dominique was a Dutch archaeologist
[31] Mohammed Jumra was the principal Arab pick man

Dutch excavation Camp – 23 March

Tonight a moon like a fall of snow; the light has no colour and the shadows are dense. In the last two days the sand has dried out white; the croaking frogs are driven to the surface, and to the lights of the camp. A slight wind makes the dark and moonlight turn to an unreal sensation of cold.

In the day a quick visit to Jerusalem under the guise of returning the theodolite to the British School. I took the road to Nablus first, and saw it vividly after a gap of one month. The faces of the Arabs travelling with me made less impression, but the Mediterranean, olive, healthy feeling of the mountains bordering the Jordan river was exciting. Flowers have sprung up all over the brown rocky earth, and ignore the power of the summer heat. Every half mile or so we pass a group of water jars alive with bees. The crops become daily more green and closer to fields of jungle grass. The exceptional rains this year will mean happiness to this countryside of farmers.

Jerusalem seems to have avoided its expected chaos of Easter week, and the Souk was as normal as ever. Perhaps the Nasser/Hussein meetings have turned away the politically more conscious of the pilgrims, or perhaps it was just the heat of the sun. The New City was shot a little with the phony sparkle of Americans, but it felt quite suited for them.

Yesterday I had spent the day surveying busily as we expected Crystal (Bennet) to come for the machine at any time, and so could work to no real plan. In the evening I drew some more flints with a slight improvement, and later read a little of a book about making films. The theoretical parts about its psychology, cutting, editing, montage, aesthetic etc. were fascinating, but the superficial reports of each nation's progress, and individualism in film making, I had to skip.

Dutch Excavation camp – 24 March

It is unreal to think of leaving Deir Alla when it has become such a home; the two cats with smeared brown patches and angry eyes, the white mother dog that looks surreptitiously after its only puppy, the heaven of losing one's skin-full of dust each evening into a muddy bucket of water, the stories of past storms and the madness of archaeologists; all these have become the background to my life.

Today the sun truly proved its power to us, and ignored the insecurity of our lives, as it baked the earth; in the summer an egg can be fried on a stone in five minutes, and one's sanity in only a little more time, but the evenings are cool at once, and the nights still cold. The rows of mended jars are always looking through me when I write, perhaps ungrateful for their resurrection and the loss of the earth's grave.

In my thoughts, I am frightened of the nomad's life with its great chances easily missed.

Hotel el-Raja, Damascus – 25 March

Plans for a film came today as I battled against the boredom of half conversation in a taxi; the idea came of combining the Osiris religion, and the murder of Kennedy into a parallel theme. Both could start with a conquest, and end in the inevitable death of the hero; both are basic to us but at the same time unreal. No-one can really accept the idea of his death; we can only accept his absence.

Today I spent mainly in travelling to Damascus and in my initial disappointment with Syria; it looks at first like a softened version of English coal mining country.

My taxi driver was curious to find out why I wanted to visit Damascus and asked me if I had come to see the hanging. He explained that three men were due to be hanged in public that day, and that this had attracted large crowds. I was glad to avoid the scene.

Hotel el-Raja, Damascus – 26 March

Fleeing rather desperately from this helpless city or perhaps from our own Western disabilities. It is a huge symbol of all that is pathetic. Jerusalem has more confidence than this chaos, and a knowledge of its own hidden greatness. The Damascus souk is unyielding in its sordity; there is no pattern and no love behind it. The buildings hold everything that remains of worth. Angular streets of sleepy sloping houses that reach out to greet each other across the turmoil underneath. Wonderful scroll shaped grills of windows, and doors simply carved, that contain only emptiness.

The Arabs can escape either to the mosque with its huge smells of bare feet and past holiness, or to their surroundings of synthetic Westernism. There is no other reality they can find to relieve the inevitability of their life.

The museum, full only with tourists, is a perfect explanation of what has passed. A fourth century synagogue is reconstructed inside; decorated with the most modern orange murals, and a hollow architecture. The Byzantine glass and the animal bronzes breathed sadly. The tomb of the crusader Sultan was erected by a czar.

DETAIL OF A PAINTING PREVIOUSLY LOCATED IN THE BASSOUL HOTEL, BEIRUT. ANONYMOUS, C. 1870. THIS SHOWS THE COASTLINE OF BEIRUT AT THE TIME. THE BASSOUL IS THE LARGE BUILDING TO THE RIGHT WITH THE FLAT-TOPPED PEDIMENT.

Perhaps in this mood I should realise that we see only the façade, but that it is too hollow to hide everything that lies behind it. Perhaps if the sun was shining and the traffic was stopped in the street...perhaps

Hotel Grand Bassoul Beirut – 27 March

At one o'clock we got to Beirut where real Gruyere can be got at a price, and the cars don't have to be American. Gertje knew the hotel; it is perfect with crumbling marble floors, and empty bedrooms painted in the Pompeian way, with just a bed and a chair for comfort. The contraption for holding my toothpaste is similar to a chandelier, but Baroque in its design and inefficiency. The central room upstairs is Turkish, with long dusty folds of tapestry on the walls, and furniture inlaid with frantic ivory. At heart though, with its friendly decadent grandness, it's mainly French like the rest of the city, and the spirit that runs through it.

A wonderful stomach reviving lunch of chicken cuscus looking out over the sea, and then on in the afternoon to wander through dusty antique shops and vivid seaside cafes. A day off, thank god, from 'official' sightseeing.

* * *

A happy fishy mood with the sea slipping angrily over the rocks and the deep Turkish eyes of a water-pipe looking at me. The café leans out,

THE SALON OF THE HOTEL BASSOUL

hopeful, over the water and a long blue balcony rests in front of it; Friday is a day for backgammon and tea in the side rooms with no women. A green mermaid rock appears sometimes under my feet, framed by the wooden palings, and magical before it hides under the next wave. We drink tea and speak forgetfully of useless things.

I have just bought a half-faded purple printed sheet that sings boldly of its age and the dreams that it loves. Loose papers and our orange peels dance in the water together; their last dance. The sun gleams towards the broken café over Beirut's rich concrete, and a boy pesters us hopefully with offers of gum. A day when we have understood about living, and are not quite sure how.

A grey smell climbs faint from the littered floor, and the empty waiter's jacket next to me. The people fish here in the English way with bamboo rods and a straggling pier beneath them. They are pleased that it is Friday, and that we share their rest with them.

Hotel Grand Bassoul Beirut – 28 March

The love of the East seems to have arrived at last, and I am starting to feel more deeply for this nomad life. Yesterday we travelled to Tyre and Sidon, where the smells of history hardly lingered, and we found little of antiquity.

At Sidon there are two small and pleasantly unforboding crusader castles; one fills an island a little way off the shore, and is linked by an almost Chinese zig-zag bridge that appears more designed to keep out devils than Turks, or maybe they were the same. The castle is craggy, and most of its remains fit awkwardly together, but there is one fine vaulted room where the fishermen keep their rods, and the castle its spirit. The depths of the sea linger there, and crawl in well scented through the narrow cracks of windows. The other castle is fascinating for its flowers, and its precarious position, surrounded by allotments and the backs of streets. A few years ago it was excavated, but of this only distorted lengths of railway track and a few rounded trenches remain.

We found the windiest and most uncomfortable rock between Tyre and Sidon to eat our lunch on, and to rest a little. My stomach disliked it as much as my bones, and we left soon. Tyre has no remains of its biblical past, and hardly any character, but we felt duty bound to visit it.

THE CASTLE OF SIDON

This morning we left the Bassoul, and the waiter, having taken great trouble with our breakfast, asked unashamedly for backshish. He seemed sorry to get it so easily. I had my stomach checked at the American Clinic, and it seems to be alright, but worried only by the constant moving. We reached Baalbek at eleven and wandered rather sadly through the Jerash like magnificence. It had temples and tourists and long long streets. Blake would have loved it for its sense of religion, and I did for its deep essential cornices and its forlorn nakedness, but it was all a borrowed glory. I have read too much of Etruscan places to be in the mood for a Roman ideal. That said, I was happy to go there.

In a ridiculously priced taxi we arrived at Homs, to a few days of touring. I prefer the villages and the country Arabs!

Freya Stark wrote about Baalbeck in a letter dated 5 May 1928
'And we came here and have a room with the ruins just opposite – big square blocks and six immense grand columns against a ridge of snow and hill. We are going after tea to look: one should take one's ruins carefully in small doses between meals'. She went on to add 'Not as good as the Acropolis, not so fine; a little more lavish decoration, just the difference between Greece and Rome'. Freya Stark Letters, Vol 1, pp 168-9

Hotel Bassan, Homs – 29 March

My arrival in Homs coincided with a major uprising against the Ba'th who had taken control of the Syrian government and army in 1963, and had in the process crushed most of the opposition parties including the Nasserites. Unknown to me at the time, a commercial strike had started in Homs in on Feb 22, and very heavy penalties had been imposed on the leaders. There was a cessation of hostilities which luckily coincided with my visit, but on April 5 they broke out again leading to the authorities shelling the Sultan mosque in Hama killing dozens of protestors. Through a complex train of events, this eventually led to Hafez al-Assad becoming the effective military leader of Syria in 1966. His son Bashar al-Assad stepped into his shoes, and on his death became president in 2000.

The Syrian countryside today was yellow, and completed its beauty with distant hazes wrapping themselves over the hills, and the occasional sight of a wild lily. The houses are stone, and sometimes of mud, but they are black and feel divorced from the land.

The valley with Homs in it has no main river but many streams, and the ground is often steep enough to be terraced. From the evenness of the

CRAK DE CHEVALIER; RECENTLY DAMAGED BY ISIS, BUT LARGELY STILL INTACT

banks of the streams we imagined them to flow always along the same routes, and the land was sown with corn right up to their sides.

Crak de Chevalier stands on one side of the valley, perched like an eagle's nest, and with a view that is bounded only by the horizon. It is a superb ragged castle that was loved as a home as much as a defence. The drive up to it winds through long sweeping terraces that should hold olive trees, but are now unused. Occasionally there was a classical pair of bullocks forlornly ploughing a narrow strip, with the music of distant children playing, and the hum of people working that came from the villages.

The castle exceeded all of our expectations of fairy palaces that wander endlessly in their own meandering logic. All day we dreamed our way through the vaulted passages, and the strong yellow shafts of light that sometimes broke through the roof. There are two levels of defences and both are sheer and impenetrable. Occasionally we found a room with a fine carved stone cornice, or a gothic chapel, but the main impression was subterranean and misty. It had for us all the magic that one hopes for in one of the greatest castles of the world.

Hotel Bassan, Homs – 31 March

I'll begin with the sunset over the desert, driving back from Palmyra, and the end of the month which has arrived so soon. The sun died sharply in a frenzy of orange and with signs of tomorrow's dark clouds, while the sky deepened its blue over our heads.

On the mountains to our right, the cloak of a black cloud was veined with pink and orange, collecting itself while the sun sinks to a red outline.

The West sky turns pale to turquoise, and its edges, where it meets the horizon, are purple. We were driving towards the sun, and the gods became still under our movement. A hill ahead turned it all to one deep line, and in a moment the glory was lost to the last brief minutes of dusk. We left the car to gather the end of the daylight, and with the cold that comes too fast, drove back with our lights on to Homs.

Palmyra was hot, and full of the desert's sand that lapped increasingly against the stark rows of columns and the bric-a-brac of fallen palaces. It was a monument to the kingdom that could oppose Rome, but built in Rome's style. Long streets that reared too confident from the eternal flatness, and a medieval castle perched romantically on the only hill. A huge struggling upright ruin that dared to live in the Bedu's domain. We reached it, amazed, over the brow of a small hill, and could have taken a day to touch every Corinthian column.

The tombs are stone square buildings that stand as sentinels in the near distances; a constant reminder of death's glory to the city dwellers. Others are nearly catacombs, but vaulted and elegant inside. The guide was right when he called it an unforgettable day, and I was unforgettably moved.

A view of Palmyra showing the castle in the background; Palmyra has also been recently damaged by Isis but recaptured by the Syrian army

A poem for Palmyra:
Emptiness,
Except for a camel's shepherd
Or a Bedouin tent
Or a violet mountain
Looking from afar.
And suddenly comes up
Palmyra...
Glorious and proud in its deep loneliness
As if a piece of an unreal world.
And you pause, breath taken
Charmed with all this grandeur
The most marvellous meeting in the desert,
Palmyra

Dutch Excavation Camp – 1 April

An early start at 6.00, and a day spent in taxis, lorries, and the Syria/Jordan customs office. Went to the post office in Homs to telegram that I was coming back to Deir Alla, and found around 50 men throwing stones at the front of it. Managed to walk round to the back where things were largely carrying on largely as normal, and sent the telegram.

This was a continuation of the uprising against the Ba'th that had started on 22 February; as a foreigner I would not have been an interesting target for the insurgenets.

From 7.00 to 9.30 travelling from Homs to Damascus. On the way encountered a tank's gun barrel coming round a corner at speed towards our taxi, but it showed no interest in us. A cup of tea in Damascus, and 10.30 to 2.00 travelled from Damascus to Swegli . An hour's wait before a lorry going to Nablus stopped for me, and I reached the camp by 3.45.

I noticed the length of the Jordanian barley, and particularly its whiskers, compared to Syrian; our valley has browned much in my week away. Now back I love being in the camp too much to be interested in going to Turkey. We have found some fine pottery, and an early inscription, that makes Henk want to lengthen the dig by a month.

Dutch excavation camp – 2 April

Made a decision to stay at the dig, before leaving for Corfu; the camp has a real sense of purpose after finding a series of alabaster jars, seals, carved objects, and an early Canaanite inscription which is really important. Terry, Dominique, Henk, Anne, Mohamed Jumra and myself are all that is left. I am curious that that the Dutch students wanted to leave so quickly, and sorry that they missed so much. There now is a feeling that one can hardly turn a spadeful of earth without its underside being made of gold.

The early Canaanite inscription turned out to be something quite unexpected. In all ten tablets were found, three of which were inscribed with texts written in a previously unknown script, and seven were inscribed only with dots. From the surrounding stratigraphy they were from the late Bronze Age, and date from before 1200 BCE.

The diary continues...

The little puppy is already losing its gracefulness, and the mother is turning over its education to its very interested father. Terry and I moved our tent in the evening to face the stars, and the evening sun; in the morning the flies should be less interested, and sleep more possible.

    I am left to manage the few workmen still left on the tell, and to continue my job as site supervisor. The difference is that the site for me to manage is now the whole excavation, and today was hopelessly busy. Henk draws sections, thinks, and is becoming more and more occupied with local officials and museum problems. Anne is bored with bare pots, but with the writing on the tablets and some faience to reconstruct, she has an excuse to forget them. Dominique has all the medley of cataloguing, sorting, and helping out jobs to do, Terry draws beautifully and makes everyone happy. I am too content to write anything more.

Dutch Excavation Camp – 4 April

The sun held us today, fixed immovably to the sweat of our bodies, and the choking claustrophobia that real heat brings. The clouds were black, scraggy blankets that let the sun collect around the valley; two hundred meters below sea level as we were, the air stifles itself, and the flocks of migrating storks bring memories of vultures and a screaming Chinese kite. Even the colours are giving themselves away to the white dust that becomes omnipotent.

TERRY DRAWING FINDS

Work's balloon puffed up to fill most of the day, and if I can surrender to it, the rain from my forehead will drip unnoticed. The layout of the room joining onto the temple, with the tablets and flower-thin alabaster vases, is almost worked out, but the nearby tangle of walls left behind by two earthquakes, and a fire that came after them, is the awful knot that really concerns us.

The children were playing a game of taxis as I walked back from the tell; they screamed bye-bye, and their eyes were asking me to join. Three dancing heads that sat in a long pig's food trough, and dared to surrender to their imagination. No wonder that dark corners hold ghosts when so many minutes can be passed in make belief.

As I lie with the tent flap open, a village in the mountain opposite jingles its light in the dark, and I imagine a ship looming out from the valley. Perhaps those children are longing to sail to the edge of the world, as I am longing to stay.

Dutch Excavation Camp – 6 April

Most of the day spent juggling with the tell, and a white Southern dust that wraps itself around everything, and our teeth. At present we are cutting a line of sections across the slope of the tell, to an old sounding of Diana Kirbride's. Two years ago a few houses and fine pottery levels came out, and it is essential to tie them in stratigraphically with the main excavation. On the way came the tablets, and tomorrow's plan is to cut deeper into the hill, through a lot of iron age material, to find the rest of their surroundings, and perhaps some more like them. We expect to have three more days digging and a frenzy of drawing sections, cleaning new pottery, taking photographs, and cursing at the weather that's showing its harsher side.

Yesterday, at half past six, I saw a small cavalcade of gypsies wandering along the road on their donkeys. There were two men who walked, persuading the animals to behave, and keep their packs from slipping over their sides. Four colourful, but not gaudy, women were riding on them, with a heap of small children that I did not notice until they came to unload. The campsite they chose had been used earlier by gypsies, at the water end of the small Arabian tell. In a moment the leading donkey was unburdened of its wriggly tent poles, and every window in the village framed a shy inquisitive person peering at the newcomers. The camp of two tents was raised, with the children being as obedient as the donkeys about not straying away. The tents were roughly cubes, made from a double layer of sacks sewn firmly together, and elegant in their simplicity.

Traditionally the gypsies live either from mending the broken pots and pans of the village they settle beside, or else by their dancing girls. Terry and I had hoped to go down in the evening to watch, but by eight this morning they had wandered on.

Yesterday two English friends of the Frankens came to dinner in a happy, familiar way; the kitchen was full of the bustle of preparation that slowly filtered to all the camp. I remember knowing by the sound of all the slops that everyone else was cleansing their skin in buckets of water. The dinner was excellent, and the sky miraculously cleared to let through the stars.

In the morning, the terrible shock of a half Mongol girl who arrived, convinced that she was going to work with us on the dig; Pekinese eyes and a fat protruding tongue that prevented her from making any understandable speech. She could hardly dress with lipstick splodged onto her cheek, and her stomach bulging from the middle of her dress. (Now I hate myself for the disgust I felt for her, and the hostility that must have come from me). Anne had the impossible task of explaining, over a breakfast of porridge and kippers, that she could not join the dig. I was so concerned that I spluttered coffee over the table, and Terry could only count the bones in his fish out loud.

With the evening, news came to us that the story of the tablets, with their inscriptions, has spread all over Jerusalem, and that a picture of them had fallen into the wrong peoples' hands. There is fear of a bandit publication before the main dig report, and anger is only just being kept away.

Dutch Excavation Camp – 7 April

Three more inscribed tablets, and a double-edged bone comb, came out from the tell today; two German professors came snuffling amiably round looking for any traces of writing, and pretended hard to be generally interested in archaeology. Terry kept them at bay, and we laughed rather cruelly at their disappointment.

The dig is becoming a fascinating puzzle, but I like it for that, and the way it is making me work. The fire that raged after the earthquake in the Bronze Age village has left some beautiful remains in our sections; strong yellow oranges fading into brown, with often a stripe of melting greens and ochre. In the evening I cleaned some sections and made 'pictures'.

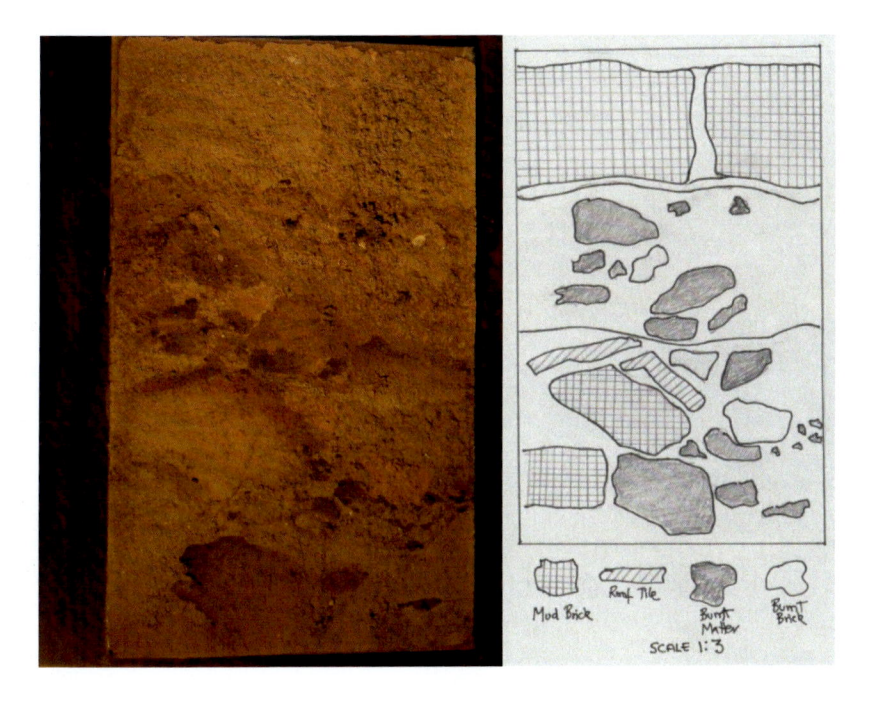

An example section showing the effects of an earthquake in the lower area with burnt mudbrick and wood, and a thin layer of fill above before building restarted, and two new mudbricks appear. Although not certain I suspect this Late Bronze Age example of destruction followed by rebuilding may have taken place at the time of a major earthquake, affecting most of Palestine, in 1365 BCE and coincided with the collapse of the walls of Jericho

These 'pictures' were made by scraping the sun-dried sections clean of any dust, and then spraying on a thin layer of glue quickly followed by a sheet of plastic. In this way a micro-sample of the section is preserved exactly as it was when it was first uncovered.

Brown dangling Hobesi covers a lot of the valley, and the corn is still standing with the wind running through it like a wave. The irrigation canals make regular snakes of water, giving a pattern to the open fields.

Two of our workmen were gamefully pushed down the steep earth tip in the afternoon, and a painless fight broke out between the foreman Ali, and an old tattooed Bedouin. They quarrel like young puppies, but love each other again after five minutes, and ended the day arm in arm.

There is little time to sit and watch the fantastically lit lorries that rush past our village; too much to be done before the dig ends.

Dutch Excavation Camp – 8 April

In a field this afternoon I found a breezy black sack of a scarecrow, standing still to look over the corn he had helped raise; the wind ruffled his hair, and his jacket flapped considerably. There are next to no birds left alive in the valley by the Arabs, so the scarecrow must have had it easy. His friend stood nearby, but blown down and crumpled. There are thorns in the ground that catch one's feet, and thistles to catch one's hand; flowers shoot from them in a violent sinister way, and a black scorpion has his hole dug reverently at the root.

Any streams dry in an hour to a maze of cracks when the water ceases to flow, and irrigation is being stifled by the approach of summer. The barley, apparently the main crop here if it can be judged by its whiskers, has only a few more weeks to stand before it is massacred painstakingly with sickles. It is high enough now for children to lose themselves in it, and open enough to walk through. I was ambushed by them on my way back to the camp in twilight. Darkness races over the mountains once the sun goes, and I must change for dinner with the Moore's.

Dutch Excavation Camp – 9 April

A massive feast is planned for the men after a day's work that revealed two new rooms and the possibility of more tablets. Yesterday the foreman Ali, and a pick-man called Moussa, set off in the afternoon to buy a sheep. In the evening it stood with its white wool upright, and a soapy washed face, in the center of the camp; we all felt a deep sympathy for this beast that chewed gently at the Hobesi, and showed dainty black hooves like the feet peering out of an Armenian girl's trousers.

Today it was slaughtered under our tree, and I saw only the heap of skin covered in flies, and a steamy bubbling cauldron. It seems that there are particular family members traditionally connected with feasts, for Moussa's wife was produced for the cooking, and a daughter, beautiful with a vivid orange skirt and brown face, fetched and carried. The bread was made first; large brown pancakes of dough that form the base of this meal. It is laid out, broken, on one metre circular tin trays, and soused with yoghurt, lemon, and butter all cooked together. On top comes a white heap of rice, and then the meat, which is boiled whole and pulled apart when cooked. A few fried nuts from melon hearts are sprinkled on top.

At the beginning of the meal a bowl of water is carried round for one's hands, and afterwards a taste of sour Bedouin coffee from a brass coffee pot with a long beak shaped spout.

We sat in groups on mattresses, and ate this hot delicious food in our right hands. With practise, it is possible to make a solid ball of bread, rice, and mutton, and flick it with one's thumb into one's mouth.

Eating was a serious matter, and to show affection and respect one feeds a friend with a choice lump of meat or a ball of rice. Sheik Abu-Feisal came, a charming self-respecting rabbit of a man, and he was delighted that foreigners could entertain in this way. After the meal, another taste of coffee and a cup of mint tea each. When the dishes were removed, a little thin halo of food was left for the dogs or the flies. It was all over in an hour and the Arabs left burping politely to themselves and their host.

Dutch Excavation Camp – 10 April

Yom-el-Jumna, the Moslem rest day, and a wind that made sitting in the sun impossible. Terry frightens me with his intellectual honesty, and the mirror he can unconsciously hold up to my own double-think. His parents live a suburban life, but he has seen most facets of society, and has spun his own slightly neurotic web out of it all. On the surface is his humour, and his fervent Irish nationalism that makes him order the Cork Weekly Examiner when in Jerusalem. He drinks as an Irish artist should, and sleeps less. He is old in years (32) for his way of life, not married, but gallant to women, and an excellent draughtsman.

Together we have been thinking about poetry ballad sheets, and of the ways a printing press could help his art. He can't sleep on windy nights, and suffers from the occasional distant sound of machine gun fire near the border, as well as his own hypochondria, which he is starting to manage. At present he also is worried by the grip that a nomad archaeological life is getting on him, and his painting; an invitation to a well-paid six-month dig at Mohenjo-Daro in Sindh is proving to be his nemesis.

This evening a three hour walk to the Jordan river and back with the sun stalling fast, and a panic about not making the camp before dark that was out of place in this lush corn-covered valley. Just before the river there is, by complete contrast, a barren duny strip of land with miniature gorges cut by wadis, and surreal hills. The river was muddy, and as low as I had seen it, but the swim made an exciting destination for the walk.

Dutch Excavation Camp – 11 April

We work on, with a few men left to scrape trowels at the hulks of two rooms. The pottery that comes out is fine, and quite different to the practical heavy ware from the rest of the tell. There is a litter of scarabs, faience beads, and cylinder seals through it all, and I am busy drawing plans, and whisking off flies, all day.

We are now working from six am through to two, and then on to four thirty, clearing the day's litter, and lifting pottery. Tea is followed swiftly by dinner at seven, and I use the gap to write this diary and wash a little. Bed is usually welcome soon after 8.30; the days always seem to be biting at each other's tails. What digging is left on the tell is now under my supervision, and I am well smitten with this life.

A VERY CLEAN LOOKING SECTION BEING GIVEN A SCRAPE PRIOR TO ITS BEING RECORDED

Dutch Excavation Camp – 14 April

Three times today it appeared that we had another tablet, but each time with a little scraping our hope vanished and it turned into a simple potsherd; work's prayer wheel still turns for most of the day, although the men work less with Ali gone.

This morning we had more visitors; Pere de Vaux and Professor Anderson, but they brought Dominique back, and some photographs of mine that showed how much more care I must take.

Dominique is less brittle now, and sweet in her intelligent way; she loves the dogs we have enticed to the camp as much as Anne does, and they are starting to have names; Lydia the tattooed lady, Um-dog, Mrs Burnt Earth, and George.

Last night I was sitting watching the stars with Terry, and after a little and our silence they started to swing and frolic with themselves, until a satellite appeared. Its motion stilled the heavens for us, and we could only gaze a little frightened until it had painfully dropped over the horizon.

I was woken too early with the commotion of donkeys breaking free from their posts in the local farm, and the barking of dogs that followed them. There is always a chorus of beasts of every kind here; England will be silent with only motor cars!

Dutch Excavation Camp – 15 April

Moussa the pot-washer cooked wild oats in a fire tonight, and the orange glow attracted us; we crouched around the embers to pick the heads and separate the chaff with our hands. The taste is similar to beech nuts, and the rasping smoke still curled around from the glow of some obstinate branches.

In the day the fields are alive with men working, and women wandering; there are always tomatoes to be picked or goats to be milked. The people take naturally to the land, and at sunset when the valley becomes empty, and perhaps a traveller is leading his camel the last few steps to the village, there is a coldness again.

When I was hurrying up the tell this morning, loaded with ridiculous bags and poles, a woman pulling a mule with a child in her arms passed by, and I felt how unnecessary we archaeologists were to the world. It's almost profane to dig up past lives, when the present is so unaltered.

Moussa has bought a black goat to sacrifice for the death of his father, and it sits under the tree where the pensive sheep was killed; the animal drives away evil spirits with its fleeting soul, and the dead man can then rest in peace.

Dutch Excavation Camp – 17 April

A very real glimpse of an earlier age came to us as we drove back from Jerusalem this evening. The plain was flat with its brown hairs of grass, and the mountains close by, and dark. Some Bedouin were camped in their black specks of tents, and the silhouetted camels grazed like wandering dinosaurs. Above the hills to the West was an unreal pink expanse of sky, and all traces of buildings were lost over the horizon and in another world.

The Nablus road is studded with ancient symbols; odd orange stones to mark the way, storage pits with mudbrick walls and pointed rooves of daub and wattle, rows of water jars making a home for bees, a Jewish rock cut tomb with a seven branch candlestick. The higher country is still a fierce green after our valley's brown, and in the city it was raining.

Dutch Excavation Camp – 18 April

Digging on the tell came slowly to a halt, like a ship just waiting for the sea to stop it, instead of using its engines in reverse; no great finds, and so no hope of any more, but some careful photographs and the promise of more relaxed mornings. In a lonely slightly delirious way I felt happy and buoyant enough to act a part with people, and not care.

Nicoletta had written a long mysterious letter that I don't understand, but she makes oneself feel huge, and herself a soft unseen Persian fountain of good. Life can be almost too much to be real, and too spiritual to exist, but it is never a necessity, only love is. Perhaps she is unbelievable in her honesty, or perhaps it is just the gemlike path that these letters lead us on. In the threads of her words there is the suggestion that some disaster has just passed, or it could be that she is over some crisis. I can only just remember her as a reality; only as the mood that she brought, and the idyllic symbol of the Piazza Navona.[32] A boy writes psalms, and a girl sings them for us all.

Dutch Excavation Camp – 19 April

The Arabs' clothes have a strong pattern that runs through the jumble of pin-striped trousers and Kufiyahs. There is an obvious distrust of any nakedness, that perhaps comes from the strength of the sun. Pyjamas are accepted as outdoor dress, and one Arab scientist, that came to England to study, collected a large crowd whilst praying on Brighton pier dressed like this.

---

[32] I had dinner in Rome with Nicoletta and my mother in the Piazza Navona a year earlier

For the poorer refugees, almost any style will do, but surprisingly on Fridays the cloth worn is often made in England, which one can see from the selvedge that they display with pride; the men keep their headdress and the women the long white scarf that covers their hair and their backs. The evening roads are made beautiful with these silent elegant figures often topped with a water jug on the way back from the well.

Old women still wear the proper traditional black that is a world-wide symbol of their state of life. The country women have thick serge dresses for the winter, made gaudy with embroidery, but quite plain in shape. As the summer comes, they turn to olive green cotton, with a matching veil.

The men, except when they are having a feast, or are a sheik, dress almost in rags; it is the art of colourful patches that enlivens them.

For the Bedu, and the rest of the Arab world on feast days, there is a sincere and stern style for men. By contrast the Armenians are largely Europeanised, but the girls often forget to take off their trousers from beneath their skirts, and the boys wear a large ugly scarf. Hats are rare, and even the army keeps the Kufiyah, on top of the usual khaki.

Dutch Excavation Camp – 20 April

We have largely mastered the technique of taking a 'squeeze' from the wall of a section in the tell; this involves painting successive layers of polyvinyl and Arborite glue onto the crumbly surface, and when this is dry and backed with sheet plastic, peeling a thin layer off like an orange skin.

At the moment it's slow work; an area of two meters by one takes rather more than a day, and we are experimenting with spraying. A well-chosen squeeze can be beautiful, with both the colours and the texture of the clay preserved, and today we took part of the transition from a burnt to an unburnt level. Tomorrow I will do one or two for myself.

In the afternoon Henk and I went to Jericho to try to lift a heavy Neolithic carved stone left behind at the bottom of the excavation. The rain started before we arrived, and the paths down were too slippery to risk carrying anything. The countryside was full of soldiers making for home, and the Eid al-Adha holiday that starts tomorrow.

There is too much mending of pots, drawing sections, taking photographs, and writing articles for the Times to let anyone think of their own packing. It will be at least two or three weeks before the camp is finally packed up, and I feel sad that I will be leaving everyone with so much to do.

Dutch Excavation Camp – 21 April

A lazy day that does not sing true, with a combination of influences; Leach's book on pottery, talking to Terry, archaeology, all linking the threads of history. It is hard to look at the threads and to realise that the spider is bound by his own web.

Dutch Excavation Camp – 22 April

Finishing off a dig is like preparing a ship for the sea; the last plates are bolted into position and the whole becomes watertight. The people see only the exterior, and little of the processes that made it, but with their limited view they can be very critical. A lot of the care that goes with the work is lost for the present under the brilliance of the surface.

Now is the time for some of the specialists to do their work; chemical analysis of building materials, comparative analysis of pottery, interpretation of the tablets by paleo-linguists, interpretation of seals, all have to be undertaken.

Today is the first day of the al-Adha holiday; almost like Christmas for the Moslems, with their feasts and the wearing of fine traditional clothes. It is a day for visits and for families.

Ali the foreman came back, darker than ever with a grey denim shirt and white kufiyah, with his sweet frizzy haired daughter to see us. One or two of the workmen came with bundles of corn burned gently in an open fire. As we worked on the tell, drawing sections and talking things over, a snake of little girls wound its way singing past us. Their clothes were too brilliant to reveal much of their dark faces, but their hands waved red claws, and heaps of bangles. We could see that they joked with their songs, but loved them at the same time, and they were happy to ignore us.

The news is black from Syria with a massacre in Homs, but with the holiday on we can find out little more. It is too easy to remember the smell of the needy crowds that filled those streets.

Dutch Excavation Camp – 23 April

My last sad, sunny day in the camp before the new world of Corfu. In the morning I tried to help Henk with drawing the sections; they were too dried out with the wind to be discernible, and so cracked open that looked more like a crossword. Um-dog came to keep us amused, and to show that it could dig holes in the ground as well as anyone else. With its love for its daughter Lydia, and its sad yellow eyes, it demands respect when it passes; Terry just cocks an eye at it.

Anne champed for fresh pastures after lunch, and we set off to tell El Saidia, and the more distant ruins of Pella. The mound from a distance

PELLA, ONCE CAPITAL OF MACEDON

looked like a Bedouin tent, but when one gets nearer the corners are rounded, and covered with purple thistles and straggles of Hobesi. The Iron-age stone staircase that runs down one side to a Wadi is very fine, and much like parts of old Jerusalem. It had been built to provide access to a water source outside the city's fortifications.

The excavation on top was at this stage quite superficial, but it is the first season, and a lot of that time has been spent on connected tombs. The site is perfect, with a sense of wildness and the Jordan river running past its foot.

Pella, one of the ancient cities of the Decapolis, was reached by a long walk over foothills where a modern village had sprung up. From the distance the shapes of a theatre can be seen, perched on the sharp edge of a ravine, and a wood grows at its feet. Some Arab boys sat with me and were happy to find a companion who loved the ruins.

Athens, British School of Archaeology – 24 April

I flew out at 7.30 in the morning from Amman airport, travelling via Beirut, and reached Athens at 2.15pm. I was welcomed at the British School that has accommodation (bare but comfortable 'horse-boxes') that is free for students. The library was very fine, and I had been given an introduction by Anne to a man named Popham who took great care of me.

Scrapbook Letters

After completing the editing of this journal, I came across a scrapbook containing the letters I had written to my parents when on the dig.

One or two extracts add some extra colour to what had been going on:

11 March 1964

I have made in the last week a five-minute film of the work on the tell, as real as possible, and probably boring, but at least one realises some of the problems. To me the camp has become horribly normal and I don't even feel much like wanting a bath, or a party, or a drink with ice in it, or roast beef, or anything particularly normal.

This week we have been overwhelmed by French actresses from Phaedra, journalists from Elle, tours of monks-to-be from Jerusalem, pinkish professors from Germany with unbelievable children, and all the other aspects of the community out here. Americans always start by introducing themselves and their professions; followed up by 'well have you found anything' which with the camp knee high in potsherds, and the tell full of L.B. walls and frantic site supervisors, usually gives one hysterics. Henk is very good at showing groups round, and it is perpetually amusing watching them trying to understand things which he invents on the spur of the moment!

18 March 1964

Yesterday I came to Jerusalem to see Diana Kirkbright about an expedition she is making in the desert in April, and she agreed to take me with her. We will be making a survey around Petra and Al Beida of possible Neolithic sites, making drawings of any flints or objects that are too big to move, and taking photographs. As nothing will be published the work does not have to be too good, and I will spend the next few days here and in Deir Alla trying to learn a little. Diana is a tough, very real, woman who knows the desert as well as any European.

25 March 2016 – Hotel el Raja, Damascus

Damascus is a great city compared to Jerusalem or Amman, but local in a way and more uncertain of itself. The Arabs here try terribly to imitate the façade of Western life, and their failure makes ten times more a stranger than in Deir Alla, which seems still confident in its own culture.

The souk here still holds a little in its architecture of what it must have had in its life. The almost Tudor houses of mud and wooden beams reach out to meet each other across the road, the fine iron grills in the lazy shape of a scroll still hang outside a window, designed only to allow the women to see without being seen. The streets are mainly cobbled and unsafe, with their litter of home-made carts and three wheeled baskets to sell the plastic paraphernalia of life.

I am frightened too by the poverty and the thought of ignoring it all in a comfortable Western way; there are still too many sights of human beings lying forgotten in the street, and children with their half-adult faces used to too much suffering. It seems a city which one cannot look at, but only feel its need.

The Frankens and the Purpose of the Dig at Deir Alla

Dr Henk Franken, (later Professor), had started his excavations at Deir Alla in 1960. He was at the time Director of the Department of Palestinian Archaeology at the University of Leiden. However, he had started his academic career as a theologian, and was initially recruited by Leiden to their Faculty of Theology to teach Old Testament 'realia' i.e. material culture. He was interested to find a material context to Old Testament narratives.

However, as a practical archaeologist, he had worked under Kathleen Kenyon during her 1955-1958 excavations at Jericho. Following that he took on a large volume of her unpublished notes from which, working with Margreet Steiner, he subsequently published numerous articles about the dig.

Henk worked for five seasons as dig Director at Deir Alla and maintained a close relationship with the site until he retired in 1978.

ANNE FRANKEN MENDING POTS

His central objective was to build a closely-detailed chronological sequence of pottery and other artefacts, based on stratigraphy, to mark the transitions through the Bronze Age and Early Iron Age; in other words, by linking finds that were deposited at the same time because they were in the same

DAME KATHLEEN KENYON

layer. Even if that layer went up and down because of buildings collapsing, earthquakes, people digging holes etc. there was greater certainty about their chronological sequence, despite similar designs being found at different time periods.

(This approach to chronology had been used at Jericho during the excavations led by Kathleen Kenyon[33] on which Henk Franken had worked, but there were gaps remaining that the dig at Deir Alla was expected to fill. This was most particularly to fill the chronological period between the Bronze Age layers found at Jericho and the earlier work (1931-1935) by John Crowfoot at Sameria-Sebaste, which covered the duration of the Kingdom of Israel from 930 BCE to 720 BCE.

It is possible to trace a succession of overlapping influences and work experiences amongst archaeologists who understood the significance of chronology. The initiator of the practice was Augustus Pitt Rivers 1827-1900 who used the development of human objects to explain cultural evolution. He took archaeology away from mere treasure hunting to a scientific approach that insisted that when excavating, all objects found are collected and catalogued.

---

[33] Dame Kathleen Mary Kenyon, DBE (5 January 1906 – 24 August 1978), was a leading archaeologist and is best known for her excavations of Jericho and Bangalow 1952-1958. She was Principal of St Hugh's College, Oxford from 1962 to 1973.

Pitt Rivers had a profound influence on Mortimer and Tessa Wheeler his wife, who excavated Verulanium using an approach that maintained a strict stratigraphic context for all finds. Also working at Verulanium was Kathleen Kenyon, who at the same time was working at Samaria).

There was also the possibility that evidence could be found of an eastern entrance of the Israelites into Palestine; strangely this was uncovered by our dig when I was there, but the tablets containing the evidence were only fully interpreted by William Shea in 1989.

The site was chosen because surface finds contained a thick deposit of Iron Age sherds, and a thinner one of Late Bronze. The position was surrounded by rich agricultural land and was close to the river Zerka (the biblical Jabboq). From the top of the Tell seven others could be seen, making it part of a major Bronze Age population hub.

Archaeologists have made many attempts at naming our site; Nelson Glueck thought it was Succoth, Henk Franken leaned towards Gilgol but, as further evidence has appeared, we are now certain that it was Pethor, home of Balaam the Prophet.

EXAMPLE OF SOME OF THE DEIR ALLA POTTERY FINDS IN THE 'WORKROOMS FOR PALESTINIAN ARCHAEOLOGY' AT LEIDEN UNIVERSITY

The Deir Alla Tablets and Plaster Inscription

This successful translation was finally made in 1989, 25 years after their discovery, by William Shea of the Biblical Research Institute in Washington DC.

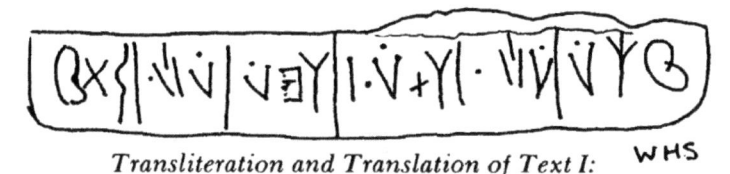

Transliteration and Translation of Text I: WHS

lkm / mk. / wtm.y / whm / mk. / ptr

(1a) "To you (have come) a smiter and a finisher,
(1b) and they (are) the smiters of Pethor."

It finally identified Deir Alla as the Biblical Pethor, which is identified in Num 22:5 (as also being the home of Balaam the prophet). This first tablet established that there had been two successive waves of attackers at Deir Alla, and the second tablet helped establish whom.

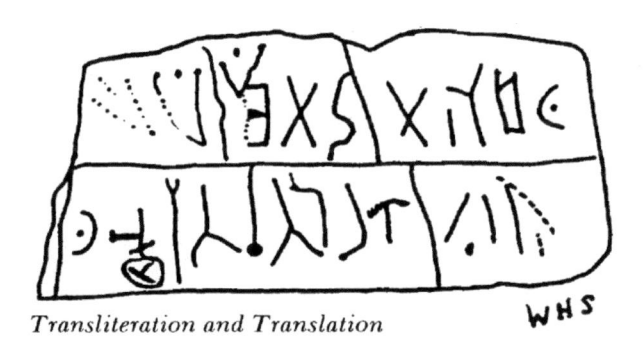

Transliteration and Translation WHS

(1) *ʿṣr / wywbbq / mk*
(2) *ʿzw ʿt / ptʾm / mk*

(1) "There was a damming up and the Jabbok (became) a smiter.
(2) Mighty (shocks) suddenly (became) a smiter."

This second tablet by the same scribe was written in boustrophedon order (both lines reading from right to left, but the lines are upside down in relation to each other).

The meaning of the second tablet has been interpreted in different ways but William Shea finally settled on '1 The mighty ones of Pithom are a smiter: 2 and Edre and Yog are a smiter'.

Pithom in Egypt was a store town built by the Israelites for the Pharaohs which they left when they exited from Egypt; it was subsequently called Ramesses but only in 1290 BCE.

(Y)Og was a non-Israelite Bashanite king who was mentioned in the Bible (Deut 1:4 and Josh 12:4, 13:12) and who would have made his attack on Pethor before the Israelites, as they subsequently defeated him and annihilated his forces and families (Num 21:33-35).

So Deir Alla or Pethor suffered two important attacks, first by a local King Og, and then by the Israelites on their journey up through Palestine.

* * *

The final, and most important inscription to be found, was revealed in 1967 when, in what was a temple area of the tell, writing on the wall was discovered in a language between Aramaic and Canaanite that can be dated to c. 880-770 BCE.

In all 119 pieces of inked plaster were discovered by Henk Franken with writing in red and black. The wall on which they were written had collapsed, presumably because of an earthquake.

The first translation was published by J.A. Hoftizer and G. van der Kooij.

Apart from the drama of the text, describing the end of the world, this inscription replicates a quotation from the Bible (Numbers 22.5) stating specifically that 'Balaam (is the) son of Beor'.

I have quoted at length below from the legible parts of the inscriptions. The Oxford Handbook of Biblical Studies describes it as 'the oldest example of a 'book' in the West Semitic language written with the alphabet, and the oldest piece of Aramaic literature'.

Balaam learns from the gods that the world will be destroyed, but somehow they manage to divert the disaster:

A PAINTED TEXT FROM THE TEMPLE AREA AT DEIR ALLA CONTAINING A PROPHECY BY BALAAM A NON-ISRAELITE PROPHET BUT MENTIONED IN NUMBERS 22-24

[i.2] The gods came to him at night.
And he beheld a vision in accordance with El's utterance.
They said to Balaam, son of Beor:
'So will it be done, with naught surviving.
No one has seen [the likes of] what you have heard!'

Balaam Reports his Vision to His Intimates

[i.5] Balaam arose on the morrow;
He summoned the heads of the assembly to him,
[i.6] And for two days he fasted, and wept bitterly.
Then his intimates entered into his presence,
and they said to Balaam, son of Beor,
'Why do you fast, and why do you weep?'

[i.7] Then he said to them: 'Be seated, and I will relate to you what the Shaddai gods have planned,
And go, see the acts of the god!'

Balaam Describes the Celestial Vision and Its Aftermath in the Land

'The gods have banded together;
[i.8] The Shaddai gods have established a council,
And they have said to [the goddess] Shagar:
'Sew up, close up the heavens with dense cloud,
That darkness exist there, not brilliance;
Obscurity and not clarity;
[i.9] So that you instill dread in dense darkness.
And - never utter a sound again!'
[i.10] It shall be that the swift and crane will shriek insult to the eagle,
And a nest of vultures shall cry out in response.
The stork, the young of the falcon and the owl,
[i.11] The chicks of the heron, sparrow and cluster of eagles;
Pigeons and birds, [and fowl in the s]ky.
And a rod [shall flay the cat]tle;
Where there are ewes, a staff shall be brought.
Hares - eat together!
Free[ly feed], oh beasts [of the field]!
And [freely] drink, asses and hyenas!'

Balaam Acts to Save the Goddess and the Land

[i.12] Heed the admonition, adversaries of Sha[gar-and-Ištar]!
... skilled diviner.
To skilled diviners shall one take you, and to an oracle;
[i.14] To a perfumer of myrrh and a priestess.
Who covers his body with oil,
And rubs himself with olive oil.
To one bearing an offering in a horn;
One augurer after another, and yet another.
As one augurer broke away from his colleagues,
The strikers departed ...

The Admonitions are Heeded; The Malevolent Gods are Punished, the Goddess Rescued, and the Land Saved

[i.15] They heard incantations from afar
...
Then disease was unleashed
[i.16] And all beheld acts of distress.
Shagar-and-Ištar did not ...
[i.17] The piglet [drove out] the leopard

The text continues but is so damaged that it is impossible to understand. However this amazing example of a prophecy by a known prophet, written on the wall of a temple, is perhaps the most exciting of all the finds from Deir Alla. And the natural imagery of how the animal kingdom would respond to a disaster can still haunt one to this day.

Postscript

At Oxford I studied Politics, Philosophy and Economics (they didn't have a course on archaeology) and then went on, as mentioned above, to found a letterpress book printing and publishing company called the Compton Press.

However, to my great surprise and pleasure, I had several years later a call from Crystal Bennett, who wanted me to travel to Jordan to meet her, and discuss the editing, designing, printing and publication of the results of a 1980 Jordanian archaeological conference held at Oxford, under the sponsorship of HRH Crown Prince Hassan.

Crystal was at that time Director of the British Institute for Archaeology and History in Amman, having been previously Director of the British School of Archaeology in Jerusalem.

I was flown out first class on Alia (Royal Jordanian Airlines) where we were unexpectedly served champagne, and entertained by aisle-hopping belly dancers.

The conference on the topic of 'Studies in the History and Archaeology of Jordan' was later repeated every three years and I was given the task of overseeing the publication of the 1980, 1983 and 1986 conferences.

The work was absorbing as it entailed editing papers submitted from around the world, organising the detail of how illustrations were to be reproduced, finding and working closely with a book designer, obtaining competitive print quotes, and overseeing the production itself.

Henk Franken continued working in Jordan for over two decades after his period of the dig closed, leading to a very close relationship between Jordan and the Netherlands.

A substantial dig house and museum has been created at Deir Alla which is now a popular tourist destination.

Excavation has continued at the site, and at surrounding tells, but no more Bronze Age inscriptions have come to light.

And most sadly we have no more prophesies from Balaam to guide us into the future.